1

Through
Trials

Other writing by Isabel Didriksen:

POPPA BEAR GETS DIABETES
1999, Duval House Publishers, now Nelson Publishers Ontario.

INSCRIBED 30 YEARS OF INSPIRING WRITERS
(Anthology) 2010, Forever Books.

PENS IN MOTION
(Anthology) 2013, Taylor Printing, Wetaskiwin AB.

POPPA FINDS PEACE
(Novel) 2014, Pagemaster Publishing, Edmonton AB.

Triumph Through Trials

Isabel Didriksen

TRIUMPH THROUGH TRIALS

Copyright © 2022, Isabel Didriksen

Scripture quotations are taken from the Holy Bible, New Living Translation unless otherwise stated, copyright © 1996, 2004, 2015 by Tyndale House Foundation. Used by permission of Tyndale House Publishers, Carol Stream, Illinois 60188. All rights reserved.

The Holy Bible, English Standard Version (ESV) is adapted from the Revised Standard Version of the Bible, copyright Division of Christian Education of the National Council of the Churches of Christ in the U.S.A. All rights reserved

Cover image from iStock

Published by Isabel Didriksen, Wetaskiwin, Canada

ISBN
Paperback: 978-1-77354-403-8
Ebook: 978-1-77354-416-8

All characters and events in this book are fictional.

Publication assistance and digital printing in Canada by

PUBLISHING
PageMasterPublishing.ca

Isaiah 41:10

Don't be afraid, for I am with you.
Don't be discouraged, for I am your God.
I will strengthen you and help you.
I will hold you up with my victorious right hand.

NLT

To Marcia and friends

Acknowledgements

Thank you to Creator God, my Lord and Saviour, Jesus Christ, for the inspiration to write Harry's story.

Thank you to Ernie Tessari and Judy Rilling for your encouragement, comments, and suggestions.

Thank you to friends who have shared their stories over the years.

Contents

Harry Moves On

HARRY OPENED HIS eyes to bright sunlight trying to shine through the grimy, fly-specked window. *Good mornin', Lord! Thank you for a new day*! He threw the thin blanket aside, sat up and rubbed his disheveled hair, grabbed his socks from the chair and pulled them on. Then he remembered his conversation with Mable the evening before.

"We don't have any more work for you, Harry. Sorry, but you'll have to leave."

Where was he going to go? Mable had said she would give him a ride to town, but what then? A small knot formed in the pit of his stomach. Being homeless this time was going to be a much different experience. There would be no alcohol to numb the loneliness, no 'bros' to offer another drink. He thought about his friends back at the shelter, but he hadn't talked to them for many months. They had been very good to him; had put up with his failures and disappointments, but somehow, he felt he needed to move on. He was almost fifty years old and he had wasted too many years feeling sorry for himself or telling people they were to blame for his problems. It was time to make some decisions for himself, and to follow God's will for his life.

He opened his Bible to the part he had been reading the day before. *Lord, help me know Your will, and help me to understand your Word today. Amen.* He had been reading in the book of Deuteronomy. Creator God was speaking to Joshua who was now leading the Israelite people. Joshua's leader, Moses, had passed on and Joshua was left all alone. Several times, God told him not to be afraid, to have courage and to go forward. It felt like a message to Harry, not to look back, but to step out in faith and trust Jesus to lead him in a new direction, *Thank you Lord. I'm determined to follow you for my future.*

He gathered his few belongings into a small sports bag, surveyed the crude cabin one last time and walked out the door. The frosty air woke him up and he pulled his jacket tight around his body. He noticed Mable leaving the side door of the house heading for her truck. He had hoped she would offer him one last breakfast, but if he wanted a ride to town, he better get a move on, or he would be walking the whole way.

He pulled the truck door open and climbed into the passenger side. "G'mornin' Ma'am."

"Well, you just made it in time. Thought you were still sleeping. I've got things to do and need to get to town early." She revved the motor and spun gravel as she made a quick U-turn in the yard. Harry didn't say anything, but he was praying. *Lord you know I care 'bout this lady a lot. She might be rough and tough on the outside, but I think she needs someone to understand her fears and loneliness.*

As they approached town, he took a deep breath and glanced at Mable. She was staring straight ahead at the road. *Lord help me!*

"Mable, I sure 'preciated how you let me work at your place all these months. You've made a difference in my life, and I thank you."

She nodded but said nothing. Harry plunged ahead.

"Mable, I want you to remember that God loves you and He really cares about you and Dave. Things are tough, but Jesus is there to help you, all you need to do is ask. He won't push His way into your life, but if you ask Him to help, He will."

They were near a farm supply business and Mable slammed on the brakes. "Well, this is as far as I'm going for now. You'll have to get out. See you around."

He was tempted to be upset but changed his mind and smiled at Mable. "Thanks for the ride. See you 'round!" He jumped out and slammed the door.

Harry was familiar with the town by now because he had caught a ride with Mable a few times. His biggest problem now was not knowing where he was going.

He stood on the corner near the grocery store and looked to his left. He saw a few old buildings and some newly renovated ones with fancy neon signs. To his right was the road that led to the little church he had attended on the occasions he was able to get to town. The folks he had met there were always kind and treated him with respect. He had felt comfortable in the group and had enjoyed hearing the preacher share from God's word. The trouble was, it was the middle of the week, and no one was likely to be at the church.

The sun was getting warmer, and he felt quite free as he walked down the 'church street'. As expected, there was no activity around the church, so he kept on walking. A few blocks later, he came to the end of the houses. Wide, open spaces beckoned to him just like in the past when he hitchhiked out of a city. That time he didn't know where he was going either, but this time he had Jesus with him, to help him every step of the way. *Okay, Lord. You know 'bout my situation. You know 'bout me needin' a job and some new friends. I'm trustin' you to show me what I'm supposed to do and where to go.*

He retraced his steps back to the grocery store and turned down the business street. He saw his reflection in the store windows but wasn't ashamed of himself like before. This time he had clean clothes, a clean sports cap on his head, and a smile on his face. He greeted the odd person that came along even if they didn't respond to him. He decided he should get a haircut, just so he would appear respectable when asking for a job. The money Mable had given him for his work wasn't going to go very far; he had to be careful how he spent it.

At the barbershop he asked if there were any jobs around town. The barber sort of frowned and shook his head. "Times are tough here, lots of people looking for work. Even the educated ones." His meaning was pretty clear, he didn't think very highly of Harry. Harry paid for the haircut and left.

This time he took a different street and noticed an old farm truck parked in front of a house. He walked a little slower, waiting to see if someone would come out. Sure enough, within a few minutes, a young guy, maybe in his 30s, strode to the truck and jumped in. Harry waved at him and walked up to the driver's side window that was partially rolled down. "Hi there, my name's Harry. I was wondering if you were going over to the next town by chance?"

The fellow glared at him at first but then rolled the window down more and with a slight grin on his face, "How did you know I was going to Southy? Why do you want to go there? That's a 'dead' town, worse than this one!" He gave a little sarcastic chuckle.

"I'd 'preciate if I could hitch a ride. I don't know that town, but I was hopin' to find some work over there. I just got laid off from a farm job."

This time the blonde, blue-eyed fellow let out a big laugh. "Work! Are you kidding me? There ain't no work over there anymore than here, and you think they're going to hire an Indian?" He said it with a slight note of sarcasm and put the truck into gear. "But on second thought, ride along if you like, you don't look so bad."

Harry grinned and ran around to the other door. "Thanks." They rode in silence for a few minutes, and then Harry ventured to make some conversation. "You got a good truck here, looks like it's done a lot of work on the farm."

"Naw, it's my old man's truck. He's had it for years. It's long past its usefulness. I just drive it now and then for when I've got an extra dirty job to do."

"Oh, a dirty job? That sounds like somethin' I'd like to know more 'bout."

The driver glanced sideways at Harry with a questioning look. "You'd be interested in a dirty job? Why?"

" 'Member – I said I needed work? Well, I bin doin' some pretty dirty jobs out at a farm, like cleanin' pig pens and chicken coops. Them's the worst. I ain't scared of dirty work."

"Maybe you can be some use to me after all. I hate going out to my old man's place. He lives clear out of town, almost an hour drive. He always wants me to come and clean his cow barn, especially after a few months of nobody doing anything. He's not too generous with the pay, but maybe if you do a good job, he might decide to like you and give you a few dollars. That would let me off the hook and I can get back to my girl. She didn't want me to go way out there today and be gone for hours. She gets lonesome, you know?"

"My name's Harry, what's your name, if you don't mind tellin' me?" Harry asked carefully. He didn't want to get on the bad side of this guy.

"Oh, just call me Joe. My old man's name is JayJay. He's pretty hard to get along with, has his own ideas about almost everything."

"I think I can handle that. The last lady I worked for was tough, but I managed to survive."

They drove in silence, going past a few farms spread out across the prairie. Cattle dotted some of the fields, but most of them were just grain. He marveled at the rolling hills, the clear blue sky but noticed there were a few dark clouds looming on the horizon.

"Looks like Creator God is getting' ready to show off some of His power. Those clouds look kinda ugly."

"What are you talking about 'Creator God'? Don't talk to me about God. I can stop right here and let you out." Joe gripped the wheel tight and stepped on the brake.

"Sorry, Joe. Didn't mean to ruffle your feathers." Harry shifted uneasily in his seat and turned to look out the window again. Joe took his foot off of the brake and gunned the motor. Harry kept thinking *Lord, help me to see why this young feller is so angry. Let your love shine through me.* He noticed several flashes of lightning in the direction they were headed. The clouds were getting darker, rolling in an ominous manner. He was thankful he was in a vehicle and not out on the side of the road. "Sure do 'ppreciate you givin' me a ride!"

Huge rain drops and a few pebble-sized hailstones hit the windshield. A crack of lightning was immediately followed by a clap of thunder, so loud it shook the truck. Joe kept driving, not saying a word. More lightning, then thunder, followed by bigger hail stones; Joe cursed over the din.

Harry was praying silently, his lips moving as he sat in awe at the power of the storm. *Please Lord, keep us safe and show Joe that you're real. I don't know how you'll do it, but you're able to do amazin' things, I'm trustin' you.*

The storm raged on, shaking and rocking the truck, until Harry thought it was going to tip over. He glanced at Joe and saw his eyes big as saucers, face white in terror. Joe stepped on the brake and pulled over to the shoulder.

No other vehicles were anywhere to be seen. There was no point trying to say anything because the noise from the hail and wind was too over-powering. Harry kept praying and nodding his head. At last, the storm moved on, leaving drifts of hail on the road.

Harry smiled weakly and tried to see how Joe was doing. Joe was still gripping the wheel, but colour was returning to his face. The angry attitude seemed to have melted along with the rain. "Wow! That was some storm! I've never been in such a storm. What were you saying about the Creator?"

"The Creator God is showin' us who's in control of this old world. Sure glad we can trust Him to take care of us. His Word says He loves us mor'n we'll ever know, we just have to let Him love us."

"Hmm..." Joe checked the mirrors and pulled out onto the highway again. He managed to steer the truck in low gear through the drifts of hail. A few kilometers ahead they were on dry road and came to a little rest stop. Joe pulled over. "Think I'll stretch my legs for a minute, got some kinks in them."

Harry jumped out too and grinned.

"How can you be so happy and relaxed? I don't mind admitting I was scared sh...."

"Well, like I said, Creator God was showin' His power to us puny human beings who think we are the kings of everything. He IS God."

"Yeah. I got the message loud and clear."

"And besides, the Creator sent His Son, Jesus Christ to live on this earth and to show us how much He truly loved us."

"I haven't heard about that before. Doesn't make any sense to me."

Harry sent a quick prayer up, stuck his hands in his pockets and shifted from one foot to the other.

"Well, it's like this. Jesus, God's Son was alive, but people hated Him, and killed Him. Three days later He was seen by many people, because He was alive agin'! God raised Him from the dead to give us eternal life. All we have to do is understand that we are sinners, that Jesus is the only One who can forgive our sins, and that we have the freedom to choose to accept His offer."

Joe pulled out his cell phone and checked the time, "Oh, oh! Better get on the road. JayJay is NOT going be happy. I was supposed to be there an hour ago."

They climbed into the truck and were on their way. He soon turned off onto a gravel road.

"Well, there's the layout just ahead. Some of the buildings are pretty run down, but JayJay won't leave the place, says his roots are there and he's not going anywhere." They drove into the yard and Joe rolled down the window.

An old man limped over to the truck. His shaggy, grey hair framed a deeply tanned, weather beaten face, with many furrows in every direction.

"Got you a farm hand, JayJay. He's wanting work, figured you could use some help."

Harry noted that most of the wrinkles were definitely not laugh lines. JayJay peered through the open window and sized Harry up and down.

"What do you mean bringing a lazy Indian out here? You know I don't have any use for those drunk, good-for-nothing scum." JayJay spat the words out in short angry bullets.

"Whoa there!" Joe held a hand up. "This one is kind of different. Why don't you at least give him a try. He says he doesn't mind doing dirty work. I thought you needed that cow barn cleaned out."

JayJay growled again, but reluctantly agreed. "Yeah, that barn is bad. You said you were going to do it. Just like you to wiggle out of a job. That woman you got in town is

nothing but bad news. I can't ever depend on you for anything anymore." He began to turn away from the truck but
changed his mind and went around to the other side to get
a better look at Harry. Harry tapped his fingers on his knee
and tried to stay calm. *Lord, you know I'm needin' a job, I'm
trustin' you to help me.*

"Well, get out and show me what you know" JayJay bel-
lowed at Harry through the closed window. Harry scram-
bled to get the seatbelt undone, grabbed his bag and quickly
opened the door. When he stood up, he saw that JayJay was
at least a foot taller than him. His angry manner intimi-
dated Harry, never mind the huge body towering over him.

"Yes, sir, I'm willin' to work for you. Don't have anywhere else to go just now."

Joe continued to sit in the truck and watched his father
yell at Harry. JayJay came around the truck again, still glaring at the world in general, and Joe in particular.

"Beats me how you think you can just dump some useless Indian off on me and then leave. You are my son. You
have a duty to help me out. Next thing I know, you'll never
be showing your face around here at all, like I don't exist."

Joe shrugged his shoulders and shifted the truck into
gear. "See you JayJay." He turned the vehicle around and
drove away, leaving Harry at the mercy of his father.

"Now, what am I supposed to do with you? Good for
nothing Indian. Did I hear you say you wanted work? I got
lots of it. Guess you'll need a room to sleep. Follow me."
JayJay started to walk to the house.

Harry hurried to keep up with JayJay's long strides.
Inside the house, Harry saw a kitchen table cluttered with
dirty dishes, left-over food, and flies flitting over tasty mor-
sels. To his left was a stairwell leading to the basement.

JayJay pointed to the stairs. "There's an empty room
down there. That's all I've got, - if you don't like it, well,
that's too bad."

Harry cautiously began to descend into the darkness.

JayJay flipped a light on and laughed an evil sneer. "Thought you .... Indians could see in the dark! Just use your great hunting skills!"

The smell of a damp and musty space greeted his nose. At the bottom of the stairs, Harry saw a large room with various pieces of broken furniture, a table under a window, a type of hide-a-bed in the corner, and a chair. An open door led into a room with a toilet, a small sink, and a small shower. A window shaded by shrubs stopped most light from entering. He dropped his bag beside the bed, took notice of where the single light bulb hung from the ceiling with a string to turn it off. That is, if JayJay didn't decide to play a trick on him and turn it off from upstairs. The chair looked safe enough to sit on, so he tested it. No creaks or wobbles. Good!

"Thought you wanted to work! What are you doin' down there, casing out the joint?"

Harry took the stairs two at a time and came face to face with his new employer. JayJay took a step back and let Harry enter the kitchen. Another scan of the kitchen revealed a mangy grey cat sitting on the windowsill, and a doorway into the living room. Tattered pictures lay on a table amid papers and dishes. *Looks like this place has been abandoned for a long time. Could use some help.*

"Okay, let's get out to the barn. I'll see how good you can work." JayJay went out the door, letting it swing into Harry's face. He shoved it open and followed across the yard to a faded red barn in need of new shingles and paint. The smell of cattle and manure greeted his nostrils as they entered.

"There's the manure fork, the wheelbarrow and the shovel. Get at it." JayJay spun on his heel and left Harry standing in bewilderment.

Where was he to move the manure to? He walked to the far end of the barn and pushed a huge door open. Outside was a mound of old manure, obviously from years past. He decided that was the spot to aim for. In a few minutes he had the wheelbarrow loaded and pushed it outside to the pile. He surveyed it and decided he would start a new one because the other was pretty high. He dumped the load and headed back inside.

He worked for a long time that felt more like a whole day. He was very thirsty and getting hungry. He remembered he hadn't had anything to eat when Mable dropped him off in town. *Guess I'll go an' see if I can get a drink and a bite to eat.* He looked at the manure in the barn and was pleased that the accumulated pile was considerably smaller.

" 'cuse me sir, can I get a drink, please?"

JayJay jumped up from his chair and scowled at Harry.

"Do you think I'm running a café here? There's the tap, get your own, you lazy Indian!

"Suppose you're thinking it's supper time. I ain't got a lot of food here, but guess I'll have to feed you something." He pointed at an old fridge beside the cupboard. "Help yourself." He turned, stomped into the living room, and slammed the door behind him.

Harry opened the fridge and found some salami, bread and butter. He looked for a plate, cup, and knife, and finally found some on the cluttered table. They weren't too clean, but he knew he'd eaten off other things that were worse. He filled the cup with water from the tap, gulped it down and filled it again. He sat down and prepared to eat, but first he prayed.

Lord, thank you for this food and this job. I'm mighty grateful. Help me to do what JayJay wants and to do it right. Amen.

The cat stretched, flipped his tail, and pounced on the table. Harry jumped but decided maybe this was the only friend he was going to have in this sad place. He reached out to pet the cat but got a hiss and a swat in return. *Never mind, seems he's not happy I'm here either.* The clock on the wall showed it was seven o'clock, time enough for him to go back and work till dark. He put his dishes in the sink and went back to the barn. It wasn't too long before the sun was setting, and he trudged back to the house. A light was on in the kitchen.

"Sir, I got a lot of that manure moved for you. Hope it's to your likin'."

JayJay sputtered into his coffee cup. "You can't have moved much you've only been here a few hours. I'll take a look in the morning. It better be good or I'll have your scalp!" He laughed at his lame joke.

"What time do you want me to start in the mornin'?"

Again, JayJay frowned at him and seemed to be lost for words for a few seconds.

"I don't plan for you to be staying here forever. You better get up real early and get the job done, then you can be on your way."

"Okay, sir. Good night and God bless you."

Harry was about to go downstairs when JayJay erupted into a torrent of cuss words, shaking his fist at Harry. "Don't you talk about God in this house! Understand? This is my place and there's no room for someone to start blabbing about God. Get out of my sight!"

Harry flicked the light switch on as he went down the stairs. He sat down on the rickety chair and pulled out the Bible from his bag. *Lord, must be somethin' you want to teach me in this place, but for the life of me I don' know what it could be. I thought Mable was tough, but she weren't nothin' compared to this here JayJay. Help me, I don' know what to do.*

He opened the Bible to some verses he had been reading before. He had puzzled about what they meant, but now when he read them again, he began to understand. It was in 2 Chronicles 20: 14-22, "The battle belongs to the Lord..." The last part was about going into battle with the singers in front of the warriors. That seemed kinda strange, why would God put the weak singers in front? As he thought about it more, a poem/song began to take root in his head. The more he thought about it the more real it became. He didn't consider himself musical, but somehow a simple tune formed along with the words. He lay down on the lumpy bed and hummed the melody. His spirit was lifted, he relaxed, and was soon asleep.

Early in the morning he woke with a start when he heard a loud thump from above. He jumped out of bed and ran to the window. He caught a glimpse of blue sky through the vines and decided it must be time to get to work. He washed his face and tried to comb his hair into some sort of neatness. At the top of the stairs he saw JayJay sitting at the table, drinking coffee with an empty plate in front of him.

"Time you got up, lazy Indian! The day is half gone!"

"Sorry sir, I don' have a clock and its kinda dark down there, didn' know what time it was."

JayJay jerked his head toward the fridge and stove, "Help yerself. I'm headin' to town – and you better stick to your job – no snooping around, you hear?"

"Ycs sir."

JayJay scraped the chair back, left the dishes on the table and headed out the door. Harry looked at the mess and decided he would clean it up before he went out to the barn. He filled the sink with hot soapy water and put some of the dishes in to soak. Then he found some cereal, milk, bread, and cheese, and sat down to eat.

Thank you, Lord! Thank you! I'm so blessed. Thank you for your forgiveness, your love, and your strength. Please help me to do my job well today, and to see JayJay as you see him, to bring some light into his life. The words and the tune he had heard the night before, came back as he ate, and he smiled to himself. *Thank you, I'll keep these words in my mind today.*

About half an hour later, he scanned the kitchen and grinned. He didn't know where the dishes belonged, but at least they were clean. The cool crisp morning air felt wonderful on his face, and he walked with a firm step to the barn. He worked all morning, stopping only once to get a drink. He hated the stench of the barn but knew with satisfaction that he was making progress. There were a couple of other cats in the barn that stayed clear of him but didn't take off when he talked to them or sang his little song. The song made the work go better and more and more words came as he sang. About noon, JayJay had not returned, so Harry decided to get himself some lunch. He found some canned things in a cupboard and sat down to eat. Just as he was finished, JayJay's old truck roared into the yard. Harry put his dishes in the sink and hurried out the door.

"What? Slacking off are you? Just as I figured, lazy Indian!"

Harry nodded but kept going to the barn, grabbed the manure fork and got to work. After a couple of hours, he stopped to rest. He guessed there was a few weeks of work to do but he was getting very tired and needed a drink of water. At the house, JayJay was mumbling to himself and throwing boxes and papers in every direction. Harry got a drink and decided to make some supper for both of them. He looked in the fridge and found some new items.

"What are you doing?" JayJay growled. "And who told you to clean up the kitchen? You ain't here to be a housemaid and cook. I can take care of myself. Get your own eats and leave me out of it."

Harry ate, put the dishes in the sink and went back outside. *Lord, how am I 'ppose to survive in this place? This here guy is nothin' but ugly. I've seen lots of miserable guys, but this one takes the cake. Help!*

Dusk was settling in fast. When he got back to the house Harry went down to his room, washed up and fell into bed.

This relationship carried on for several days. One morning, Harry woke up early, read his Bible, prayed, and trudged up the stairs. JayJay was not around. Harry looked out the window and saw the truck sitting where it had been parked the day before. He decided to look in the living room. He saw clothes, papers, and boxes strewn everywhere. He called out to JayJay but there was no answer. He carefully stepped through the mess toward the hallway where he presumed the bedrooms and bathroom were. He warily poked his head around the corner and called JayJay again, still no response. Then he heard a slight moan but wasn't sure where it was coming from. He went to the first bedroom, no furniture, nothing. Down the other way, he saw a closed door. His hand shook as he reached out to rattle the knob and called again. A moan, barely audible came from behind the door.

"JayJay, are you okay? Do you need help? "

Starting Over – Again!

ONE MONTH LATER

A cold wind whipped dust and debris through the empty alley. Harry pulled his jacket closer and walked out on the sidewalk. He noticed a native guy huddled up against a vacant building and decided to go over and talk to him.

"Hi, Bro, how are you? Haven't seen you 'round these parts before. Where you from?"

The man didn't answer, just sat there, and stared straight ahead, as if he hadn't heard a word. Harry slowly lowered himself to sit down next to him and said nothing more. The cement block was icy cold. Harry shifted his weight a bit to find a more comfortable spot. They sat for several minutes, watching garbage swirl down the street. A few people hurried for shelter.

"How about comin' with me to the café over there? I'll buy you somethin' to eat. My name's Harry and I know how it is to be homeless and have nothin' to eat."

The man pulled his collar up higher and held his gaze straight ahead. Harry wondered if the man was deaf, drunk, or just ignoring him.

He decided to try again, put his hand on the man's shoulder and made his offer again. "C'mon with me, I'll get you some hot coffee an' some grub." After a few more minutes of silence, the man shifted his eyes and looked at Harry.

"Why are you botherin' with me? Why don' you just move on?"

" 'Cause I know what it's like to sit on a street corner and be cold and hungry. I bin there myself."

"Good for you. What's that to me? After I eat, what then? I come back to the street corner and freeze?"

Harry thought for a minute about his former life on the street. Now he'd been living in this place for a while - ever since JayJay had gotten sick. He had found odd jobs in some of the small businesses, and even found a church where he could meet other Christian brothers and sisters. A couple from the church had provided room and board for him, for which he was very thankful. One of the sermons the pastor gave just the week before, stood out in Harry's mind. The pastor told how the church was wanting to reach out to those who were homeless, suffering from addictions, or just having a hard time surviving. Harry felt the Lord telling him to take a look around him. To actually 'see' those in need. That was when he had walked down the street and saw a 'bro' sitting in the alley.

"Jesus cares about you! I care about you! Jesus has sent me here to show you there is hope. Hope for a better life. Hope for the future. By the way, what's your name?"

The man squirmed a bit and looked at Harry again. With a reluctant shrug he said, "Al, but mostly I'm called 'Ally'."

"Well, Ally, glad to meet you. Come on, let's get a move on, before we freeze to death!"

Harry raised his body up with difficulty. He was getting old! His bones didn't like sitting on cold sidewalks. He held out his hand to Ally and helped him up. Harry noticed the man had very long legs and stood quite a bit above him. The man's jeans were ripped and filthy, his light jacket no match for the cold wind. Ally's face was tanned and wrinkled by the many cares of life. His dark brown eyes looked dead. His matted, black hair stuck out beneath an old baseball cap. Together, they watched for traffic and made their way across the street to the café.

Harry pushed the door open and felt the welcome rush of warm fragrant air. His mouth watered at the aroma of bacon and eggs. Harry guided Ally to a table for two in the corner. Other customers were giving them looks of disdain, almost saying with their eyes that Harry and Ally didn't have any right to be in *their* café. Harry ignored them and focused on Leda as she came over to get their order. He liked Leda. Her blue eyes always seemed to be sparkling.

"We'll start with coffee, please." Leda walked back toward the kitchen to get the coffee.

One of the customers motioned to her, "Why don't you throw those dirty guys out? They don't belong in here." Leda looked at the man, "If they can pay for their food, that's all that matters. They have a right to be in here just as much as you."

With that she went through the swinging door to the kitchen.

A low murmur erupted from the guys as they scraped their chairs back from the table, stood up, and pulled their coats on in a hurry. All four of them headed for the door.

Leda came back from the kitchen at that moment and yelled, "Hey! You guys didn't pay for your coffee! Come back here!" But they kept on going out the door. One of them retorted, "If you want 'those kind' in here, we aren't coming back. Too bad. *You* can pay for our coffee!" The door crashed behind them.

Harry felt bad for Leda and the way the men had treated her. "Well, guess that shows where those guys stand, eh? Sorry we've caused you trouble. I'll pay for their coffee."

He looked at Ally and saw anger smoldering underneath those dark eyes. Harry knew that feeling.

"Hey, Ally, we came here to eat! What'll you have? Leda can get you something off the menu. How 'bout the breakfast special? Eggs and toast?"

Ally continued to sit there looking ready to explode. "Why should I eat? It's no use to fill me up and then leave me on the street again. Leave me alone! I ain't worth nothin' to nobody!"

Harry's mind was instantly taken back to his days on the streets when he was homeless and hungry. He saw himself sitting near a dumpster trying to curb the hunger pangs that gnawed at his middle. How he had given up any hope of changing his life for the better. He remembered Marlene, the 'angel' who had come into his life for a short time. She was the one who told him about Jesus and His love. He also remembered how he had told her she didn't know anything and to leave him alone. Then the guys at the Shelter had helped him out in so many ways he couldn't even count them.

Ally shifted on the chair, shrugged his shoulders and settled back down. Harry motioned to Leda that they were ready to order. He ordered the breakfast special for both of them. Leda nodded and headed to the kitchen.

"You know what? I been in your shoes before. I used to sit by the dumpsters hopin' someone would throw some good left-overs in so I could eat for the day. Sometimes the pickings were purdy scarce. I'd be so hungry I could hardly stand it. I'd beg on the street but nobody would help. My life was heading for death."

"So? What's that to me?" growled Ally. "You got your life sorted out, bully for you! My life ain't worth savin'."

Harry knew it was no use arguing with Ally, but he knew he could pray. He sent a silent prayer up *Jesus, help me! Help me say the right words that will get through to this guy.*

Leda brought their plates and offered more coffee. "Someone at church told me you stay with Ron and Betty in their basement, right?"

"Yes, they've been so kind to me, don' know how I woulda survived without them. They sure know how to put the love of Jesus into action! After the scary time out at JayJay's farm, I was pretty well homeless again."

Leda's eyebrows went up. "Oh? What happened at JayJay's farm? I've heard he's a miserable cuss who hates Indians."

"That's true. That is, 'til he nearly died. I was out there helpin' clean up his cow barn. Stayed in his basement. One day I couldn't find him. His truck was there, but he didn't seem to be around. I searched through the house and found him in a back bedroom lyin' on the floor. He was moaning but couldn't seem to talk. I tried to help him onto the bed, but he was too big and heavy for me. I panicked, then prayed out loud, right there where he lay, even though he had warned me not to talk about God or my faith from the first day I arrived. There was no other way. I HAD to pray. I said, "Lord Jesus! Help! Help me get some help for JayJay, Jesus, I know you love him and care about what happens to him. Help!""

"I stood up and told JayJay I was going to get help. He moaned again and shook his head. Like he was tellin' me to leave him alone – not worth getting help for him. I told him his life was important and that Jesus loved him. I went back to the kitchen and looked around for a phone. Beside the phone was a tattered piece of paper with some names on it. I saw the name "Joe" at the top of the list. I figured that must be JayJay's son who had brought me out to the farm. My hands were shaking as I tried to dial the number. It rang and rang. After about ten rings, a man's voice came on the line. I tried to tell him JayJay was laying on the floor and couldn't talk or nothin', but he wouldn't believe me, insisted he'd seen his dad in town the day before. I kept beggin' him to call an ambulance so he finally agreed."

All the while Harry was telling Leda the story, Ally sat with his head down, poking at the food on his plate. When Harry stopped to take a bite and a slurp of coffee, Ally looked up at him and Leda. Question marks emanated from his eyes as if to say, *What kind of people are these anyway? Talking about Jesus like He was a person or something'.*

"Well, don't leave me hanging in the middle of the story! What happened?" Leda exclaimed. She noted that no one else had come into the café, so she had time to listen. She stood there with the coffee pot suspended in the air, waiting.

"You know what? Jesus really does answer prayer!" Harry had a huge grin. "I went back into the bedroom to tell JayJay help was on the way. He nodded but didn't shake his head. I sat on the floor beside him and sang the little song the Lord had given me while I was cleaning out the barn. I'd never written a poem or nothin' ever before, but guess it was given to me for a reason, for such a time as that. The words were about God's love and faithfulness to me through the hard times."

"Can you sing it now? I'd love to hear it!"

"Naw, my singin' ain't pretty and it would sound silly in this place anyway. I think it was meant for JayJay only."

"What happened next?" Leda demanded.

"Within a half hour I heard an ambulance siren come into the yard. I told JayJay help was here and rushed to the back door and waved at the ambulance people to come quick. There were two hefty guys. I was glad, because they would need all their muscle power to lift JayJay off the floor. They came into the kitchen, and I showed 'em through the clutter to the back bedroom. They used their medical equipment to check out JayJay's condition and then nodded at each other. They had a tough time hoistin' him up onto the stretcher and it took them a lot of fancy moves to get him out of the house. Just when they were drivin' away, I saw Joe arrive in a cloud of dust. He stopped to talk to the driver for a minute and then spun his wheels. I thought he was goin' to take off after the ambulance, but he came to the house, slammed on the brakes and jumped out. He admitted I had told him the truth and decided he couldn't leave me there alone, so gave me a ride to town."

Harry continued, "That's how I got to be here in Cortina. It's not a bad place. Good people here."

Ally had been sitting at the table, staring down at his food, but obviously listening to Harry's story. Leda realized she hadn't been doing her job and scurried away to the kitchen. Harry watched as she walked away. For some reason, he felt attracted to Leda. The way she walked showed a determination in her step; like she had a purpose in life. He liked that. He liked her light brown hair too and her blue eyes. Those eyes! They were amazing! Like the deep blue sky on a clear day. *Yep, she's a real gem!*

He was jarred out of his daydream by Ally coughing and sputtering in his coffee cup. Ally looked like he was choking but then recovered his breath.

"Sorry. Yer story was a bit hard to take. How can you be so sure that this Jesus guy is takin' care of you? You sound like one of those daydreamers that go on 'bout trusting in God and everythin' will go along fine. I tried that. It don' work!"

"Ally, I know how hard it is to trust God. When I was on the streets, I didn' trust nobody. All my life people had let me down. Whenever I began trustin' someone, they either stole my stuff or they lied about helpin' me. Even when I was a kid, I couldn't trust my uncles or older brothers because they hurt me real bad. So, when someone came along and told me that Jesus loved me, and I should trust Him, I just laughed. If I couldn't trust a person I saw with my own eyes, how could I trust this invisible Jesus? But then a guy named Leo kept talking to me. Over and over, he told me Jesus loved me and Leo showed me by his actions what real love was. He put up with my anger and rebellion and pride and kept pourin' God's love on me until I couldn't fight no more. He helped me understand that God loved me so much that He sent His only Son to this broken, sad world to show us in real life that Jesus loved us. Every human being alive is not good enough or can ever do enough good things to get into heaven. It's like beatin' our head against a brick wall, all our tryin' gets us nowhere and then we give up hope. That's your problem, you've lost hope."

"What's there to hope in? Another day – another day of hunger – another day of being cold, another day of loneliness? Your right, I have lost hope."

"In God's Word, the Bible, He tells us about how Jesus is our only hope for this life and for the future. He is the way, the truth, and the life. He died for your sins and mine, but He came alive again after three days. Many people saw Him in person and told their friends and family that Jesus was alive. And you know what? Jesus is alive today and He cares about you Ally. More than any human being could ever care. When you tell Him you're sorry for your sins and ask Him to help you, He will. He will make you a new person inside and you can know for sure that you'll go to heaven when you die."

Ally pushed his chair back from the table. "Bah! I don' need you preachin' at me! You're crazy!" He stood up and headed for the washroom while he had the chance.

Harry bowed his head and prayed, *"Lord, you know who this guy is and how he needs your love, please help me to show him your love in a real hands-on way."* Harry thought for a long time. Maybe he could take Ally to the church and see if the pastor had any ideas of what to do for him. Pastor Nick had been a real help when Harry needed a place to live and get a job. He thought about where he was living and wondered if Betty and Ron would be able to find someone else who could take a homeless guy in. That was a huge request. Not many people were able or willing to take in a street guy. Pastor Nick had taken Harry into his own home for one night and listened to Harry's story. The next morning, Pastor Nick had been all smiles at the breakfast table and told him he had talked to a guy that had a small business. He needed someone to help in the lumber yard, to organize the loads when they came in and to help the customers when they picked up supplies. He was willing to give him a chance. Harry had been speechless, wondering if the Lord wanted him to stay in this place?

Ally came out of the washroom, his face and hands a bit more presentable than when he came into the café. He hesitated. Harry sensed the battle going on in Ally's mind.

"How about I get a 'go-bag'?" Before Ally could protest, Harry motioned to Leda. She had heard the conversation and came over with a small bag for the leftover meal.

"Oh, here, I'll pay you for the breakfast and the coffee those guys didn't pay for, then we'll be on our way." He took the bag from Leda and went back to Ally.

"Come on, let's go down the street to see a guy I know. A guy that actually cared about me and what happened to me." He put his hand on Ally's arm and guided him to the door.

Harry pointed to the next street and urged Ally to follow him. Ally shrugged his shoulders and decided he had nothing to lose. They walked about three blocks into a residential area. Some houses were neat and clean, but most others begged for repairs. Garbage was strewn in the yards; toys and car parts were piled up against the picket fences. The picket fences indicated the former tenants had been proud of their residence and had taken care of it. *Just like people's lives. God makes our bodies all neat and clean when we enter this world. But then we take things into our own hands and ignore all the beauty around us. We dont take care of our bodies. Abuse them with alcohol and drugs and bad food; disown our families and end up with garbage heaps strewn throughout our lives.*

"Here we are, Ally. This is the place where my friend Nick lives." (he avoided calling him 'Pastor' Nick). They walked to the backdoor, Ally shuffled behind. Harry strode confidently up two steps and knocked on the door. He waited, but no answer. He knocked again, this time a little louder. Still no answer. *Hmm, I see Nick's car through the window in the garage, a baby stroller parked near the side of the garage. Wonder where they are?* He turned and looked at Ally. Ally looked like he was smirking, as if to say, *I told you so. Nobody wants a bum like me.* Reluctantly, Harry turned and stepped down to the broken sidewalk. "Guess we'll have to find somewhere else to go. I can bring you along to where I work. Maybe you could hang out there till later in the day."

"Naw, just leave me alone. I don' need your help anyway." He turned his back on Harry and started walking down the opposite street.

Harry stood there, not sure what to do. He knew if he pushed too hard, Ally would never let him come near again. He waited until Ally got to the street and started back toward downtown.

Harry made his way out to the street and turned right, intending to make it to the lumber yard before the boss noticed he was a bit late. He looked at his watch and realized he still had the 'go-bag' in his hand and that he was more than a bit late. He was over an hour late. He had forgotten about time when he was trying to help Ally. Now he was in big trouble. The boss had been very kind to him since he had been working there. In fact, he had even given him a slight raise, saying he was pleased with his work and saw him as a good employee.

What am I gonna tell Percy? I've let him down. That's not good. Lord, you know I was tryin' to help Ally, I need some help – again!

FIRE!

WHEN HE GOT near the lumber yard, his heart began to race, and his hands got all sweaty. *No point delaying the inevitable. Better get it over and done.* He pulled the door open that led into the sales area and looked around for Percy. No one was in the front part of the store.

He looked at the 'go-bag' still in his hand, meant for Ally, and decided to put it in the microwave to keep it warm. He walked to the back of the large building and went into the lumber storage area. He looked but couldn't see anyone. *Strange. There's always somebody around. Where was Trudy? How come the door was open?*

"Hello? Anyone here?" he yelled. His voice echoed in the rafters. *Don' seem to be anyone around, I'll just get busy and carry on where I left off yesterday.* He tossed his heavy jacket over a nearby railing and put on his gloves. He went to the far corner of the building and began sorting and piling the smaller boards in one spot and the larger planks in another, just like Percy had instructed him. He was finished in a few minutes and was still wondering where everyone was. He moved over to the next section and began getting a pile of lumber ready to be loaded onto the forklift. He knew a customer had ordered it a few days ago and was coming today to pick it up. That task finished he went back to the door that led into the store. When he pulled it open, he was met with a cloud of smoke.

"Percy! Where are you? Percy! Percy!" Harry tried to see through the smoke and saw Trudy groping her way toward him.

"Trudy! Over here! I'll help you!" Trudy stumbled to Harry and fell down in front of him. He grabbed her arm and lifted her up.

"Here, hold on to me! Let's get out of here. Quick!" He pulled her to the door and struggled to get it open. It finally gave under his strong arm and they both fell out onto the back parking lot gravel. Trudy was coughing and sputtering, trying to get her breath. Harry coughed and coughed; the smoke was choking him.

"Trudy! Where's Percy?? When I came in, he wasn' 'round. What happened to him?"

Trudy rubbed her eyes, wiped her nose on her sleeve, and coughed again. "I don't know! He wasn't here this morning when I opened up the store. I just thought he was with you picking up a returned order or something."

"No, I was an hour late. I didn' see you either when I came in. Where were you?"

"I wasn't feeling so good, so I was sitting in the bathroom, trying to keep from heaving up my breakfast. When I came out of the bathroom, I smelled smoke, but before I could call for help or pull the fire alarm, the smoke got too much, and I had to run for it. I'm so glad you were there to help me."

They watched helplessly as smoke billowed upwards. They heard sirens and knew that somebody had called for help. They rushed around to the front and waved at the men hurrying into the building.

Harry yelled, "We don' know where Percy is! Maybe he's still inside! Look in his office near the side door."

Harry and Trudy were coughing; both of them were shivering, their teeth chattering uncontrollably. Someone from a business next door came and threw a blanket around their shoulders and tried to reassure them everything was going to be alright. Harry couldn't stop coughing, then he felt his knees getting weak. Next thing he knew; he was on the ground.

The Dreaded Hospital

"SIR! WAKE UP!" He felt someone shaking his shoulders and managed to get his eyes open. He saw a nurse standing over him, a look of concern in her eyes.

"I've got to find Percy! Let me up! Percy is in there somewhere! It's my fault, I shouda looked for him right away."

"Sh... Sh... Percy is okay, they found him, he's going to be fine. Just rest now. Everything is okay." She patted his shoulder and pulled the sheet up over him.

Harry shivered and let out a long sigh. *Just as long as Percy was okay, that was all he needed to worry about.* He closed his eyes for a few seconds and then tried to sit up again.

"Wait a minute. Where am I? How did I get here and why am I here?"

The nurse came over to the stretcher again and talked to him in a soft voice. "You were overcome by smoke, and you passed out. The paramedics brought you in. Now try and rest. We'll see how you are in a little while, maybe you can go home soon."

"What about Trudy? Is she okay?" Harry couldn't rest until he knew Trudy and Percy were alright.

The nurse asked, "Who's Trudy? We don't have anyone by that name here."

Harry struggled to sit up but started coughing again. "Let me out 'o here. I'm fine. I got to check on Trudy. She works in the same place I do. She was standin' beside me."

"Sir, please lie down! I'll find out what happened to the lady. I can call the paramedics."

A coughing spell took over and Harry was forced to lie down on his side. *Lord Jesus, help me! Help Trudy! You know where she is. Please take care of her.* He caught his breath but started coughing, worse than before. The nurse came and put an oxygen mask on his face and told him to breath in a few times. He took some long breaths, but that set off more coughing.

"Here. Here is some medicine that will help you to stop coughing. Smoke can be very bad. When it gets into your lungs it takes a while to get it out." She helped him sit up to take the bitter liquid in between sputters and coughs. She told him to swallow a pill that would help him rest. He felt a bit of relief and lay back on the pillow and went to sleep.

When he awoke, he looked at the clock on the wall and saw it was on eight, but he didn't know if it was eight in the morning or the night. He made an attempt to sit up, but a nurse came rushing over, telling him he needed to rest.

"I've had enough rest! I need to get outta here! Call the doctor!" Harry yelled at the nurse.

"Yes, yes, I'll call the doctor. Just lie back again for a few minutes until I can get him to come." She patted his shoulder and smiled a reassuring smile.

After what felt like an hour, the doctor came at last.

"Well, sir, you've had quite a time. That smoke was very toxic, it can do a lot of damage to your body."

Harry looked up at the young guy that didn't look old enough to be out of high school let alone call himself a doctor.

"Listen to me! I gotta get outta here! I don' need anythin'. I'll be fine!" With that he made another attempt to get off the stretcher.

"Okay sir. Let me help you sit up." The nurse put the side rail down on the stretcher and offered her hand to him. With the help of the nurse and doctor, Harry managed to sit up on the stretcher and dangle his legs over the edge. His head felt a bit dizzy, but he wouldn't admit it, he was going to get out of this place. Hospitals were scary and he wasn't about to lay here and let them boss him around!

"Can we call someone to come and take you home? Do you have a family member nearby?" The nurse was really getting to him with her sickly, sweet manner. *He needed to get away from her and this place.*

"I don' have any family, just let me out. I'll find my own way home. Where's my jacket?"

"Here's your jacket. You'll have to sign this paper saying you are leaving without the doctor's permission. Dr. Thomas thinks you should stay for a while longer to make sure your lungs are not going to be damaged from the smoke."

"My lungs are fine, let me out!" Harry grabbed his jacket and stood up beside the stretcher, clutching the side to steady himself. The nurse handed him a clipboard with a paper on it. He glanced at it and scribbled his name across the bottom.

"There! Are ya happy now?" He turned and walked shakily down the hall, searched for the door, and went out into the gathering darkness. He didn't understand why he was so angry. What had happened to him? He heard a car approaching but ignored it. Next thing he knew, the car stopped, and someone jumped out.

"Where do you think you're going old man?" A middle-aged man dressed in a dark sweat suit and a bandana on his head looked rather intimidating, but Harry couldn't get around him, no matter how he tried.

"Let me get on my way."

"Harry, is that you?" The man looked into Harry's face under a streetlight.

"Harry, it's me, Pastor Nick. Are you okay? I was looking all over for you. They said you were at the hospital, but by the time I got there you were gone. Come on, get in the car. You've had a rough day."

For some reason, Harry couldn't remember who Pastor Nick was and he couldn't remember where he knew him from. *Did I go to church? How come I would have a pastor as a friend?* His mind was all mixed up, he couldn't think straight. Something was wrong. Harry decided that Nick looked like a nice guy, so he allowed him to help him over to his car and watched as he opened the passenger side.

"Here, get in. You need to come with me. You aren't yourself."

"Yeah, you're right 'bout that. I don't even know who you are! Should I know you?"

Nick had got behind the wheel and was adjusting his seat belt when Harry came up with that question. He switched the interior light on and looked closely at Harry. There were smudges of dirt on Harry's face and hands, his eyes were red and swollen. Harry started to cough and couldn't stop.

"Maybe you should be at the hospital Harry. You don't sound too good."

"No way! I ain't gonna go to that scary place! They don' know what they're doin'. A guy could die in there. Leave me alone!" Harry reached for the door handle and was getting ready to jump out. Nick managed to get his seat belt unbuckled, opened the door and raced around to the other side of the car just as Harry was almost out of the seat.

"Harry! Please let me help you! Don't you remember coming to my house and to the church when you first came here to Cortina? You've been faithful to attend every Sunday and to help wherever you could. There was a fire at the lumber yard where you work. Do you remember that?"

Harry frowned at Nick, trying to understand what he was talking about. *Me go to church? When did that happen? I'm homeless. And when did I ever have a job at a lumber yard?* Harry sat and puzzled over that for several minutes. Nick was still talking about things Harry couldn't remember. He was getting scared - real scared. He looked at his jacket and pulled his arm up to smell the sleeve. Sure enough, he could smell smoke. He rubbed his eyes because they were burning and then began coughing again. *Maybe this Nick guy knew what was wrong with him.* He settled back into the car seat and allowed Nick to do up the seat belt. Nick went back around the car and opened the door. Harry was sitting quietly so Nick did up his seatbelt and turned the key in the ignition. The motor sputtered and groaned, but after a couple of tries it came to life. They drove in silence until Harry had another coughing spell.

"I think I need some cough medicine or something, this cough don' wanna quit."

"It's from the smoke, Harry. The smoke was so thick you collapsed on the ground and the ambulance took you to the hospital."

Harry listened but still couldn't make any sense out of the story. His mind was whirling, chasing thoughts and ideas around like a rabbit escaping from a fox. Every path ran into a dead end.

"Here we are at my house. You just stay put for a minute while I go and tell my wife we have a visitor." Nick touched Harry's knee with a reassuring pat and got out of the car. Harry watched him go up the sidewalk to the back door of the house. He looked at the other houses on the street and noticed most were in rough shape. He tried and tried to pull up the memory of this place. Nick said he had been there before. In the middle of his mind search, he had another coughing spell. He was getting worn out from all the coughing. He didn't know what to do. He decided that he would let Nick and his wife help him out. He felt like he didn't have much choice.

"Rhonda says for you to come on in. She'll put an extra plate on the table for supper."

Nick was holding the door open and undoing the seatbelt. He pulled on Harry's arm and helped him stand up. Harry was shaking and weaving from side to side. Nick put his arm around Harry, who was a bit shorter, and guided him to the house. He managed to keep Harry on his feet as they got to the back door. Harry saw a lady standing in the open door. She was medium height with short dark hair and was smiling, encouraging him to come in.

"Haven't seen you for a while, Harry, it's good to see you. Come in, I hear you've had a bad day." Rhonda reached out and clasped his hand between her two hands. "Would you like to wash up before we eat? Come, the bathroom is right over here." She led him to the bathroom door and turned on the light for him.

Harry seemed to hesitate, like he didn't know what he was supposed to do, then he walked in and closed the door behind him. Rhonda went back to the kitchen. "What's wrong with him? It's like he's in a daze or something."

"When I heard about the fire down at the lumberyard, I took off right away to see if Harry was inside or if he had managed to get out. There were a lot of people standing around and the ambulance was there. I didn't see who they put into the ambulance. I heard somebody say that Percy, the owner, wasn't around. By that time the firemen had got the fire under control. There wasn't very much damage, mostly smoke. I was going to ask someone if they had seen a native guy come out of the building, but the crowd was beginning to move on to more important things in their day. I decided I'd better look for Harry. As I was driving down the street over by the hospital, I spied him walking like he was drunk. I wasn't even sure it was him, but I pulled up beside him and saw it was Harry. When I got out and talked to him, he acted like he didn't know who I was and kept talking crazy. He was ready to fight at the drop of a hat, but I managed to convince him to get in the car. He's been coughing a lot."

They heard Harry coughing and coughing and wondered if he was even going to catch his breath. At last the door opened and Harry came out, his eyes all red and he continued to cough.

"Here, Harry, sit down. Maybe if you take a drink of this hot tea, it will help stop that cough." Rhonda handed Harry a big mug of steaming liquid.

He took a sip but slammed it down on the table and shouted, "What are you tryin' to do? That's too hot! I can't drink that! Let me outta here! I don' know who you are, and I got to get goin'." He started to stand up.

Nick ran over to Harry and touched his shoulder. "Sorry, Rhonda didn't realize it was so hot. How about one of these fresh biscuits? You'll feel better if you eat something."

Harry looked at the biscuits and then at Nick. He decided to sit down on the chair and reached for a biscuit.

"Here, have some of Rhonda's homemade strawberry jam and some butter. But just a minute, I'm going to ask God's blessing on this food. We are so thankful to have food on the table and thankful having you, Harry, as our guest. Nick bowed his head and said a short prayer.

Harry watched Nick with interest. There was something about Nick that seemed to ring a bell in his memory from some time in his past. He wondered about it briefly but didn't have time to search out that thought any fur-

ther because Nick was done praying and helping himself
to the biscuits and sliced ham. He handed the plate across
the table. Harry took one slice and put it on his plate. He
glanced at Rhonda, hoping she wasn't mad at him for yelling at her. He hadn't meant to yell; it just came out. They
ate in silence for a bit.

"Harry, were you at the lumberyard when the fire started? Is that why you're coughing so much? Can you remember what happened?" Nick concentrated on his food, waiting for Harry to talk.

"I don't know what happened. It's like I can't 'member
anythin'. Why would I be at the lumberyard?"

"Well, you have a job there. When you came here, you
needed a job and a place to stay. Another fellow and I helped
you get a job at the lumberyard and found you a place to
live. You've been working for about a month and doing really well. Before that you had been working on a farm, but
the owner got sick, so you had to leave. Do you remember
anything about that?"

  Harry munched on his biscuit thoughtfully. Maybe
this guy knew something about his life that could help him
put the pieces together. The telephone interrupted the silence. Rhonda pushed her chair back and walked over to
the phone sitting on a small desk. She picked it up while
keeping a sharp eye on Harry at the table. She wasn't sure if
he would erupt into another tirade of yelling if something
ticked him off.

"Hello? Hello? Who is this? Oh, is that you Percy? Are
you okay? So sorry to hear about the fire. You're looking for
Harry? Well, as a matter of fact, he is here. How did you
think to call here? Oh, yes that's right. I agree with you
there. Did you want to talk to Nick? Here Nick, it's Percy."
She handed the phone to Nick who had come to stand beside her.

"Hi Percy. Are you okay? Oh, glad to hear that, we were worried about you too. I saw Harry walking down the street over by the hospital, so I brought him home to give him something to eat. Why don't you come over? He seems to have some kind of memory loss, can't figure out a few things. Fine, we'll see you in a couple of minutes." Nick sat down at the table and resumed his meal.

Harry sat back and heaved a satisfied sigh, "That was mighty fine!" He downed more tea. "Sorry, I didn' mean to yell at you, must be out of my mind, I know it's not nice to yell 'round a fine lady like you."

Rhonda smiled and nodded, "Thanks, I know you didn't mean it. We can move on and talk about something else. You have a nice little basement suite over at Ron and Betty's. Can you remember where that is and who they are?"

Harry looked at her with a blank stare. *What is she talkin' about? I don't know who Ron and Betty are!* He heard someone knocking on the door.

Nick went to open the door. "Come in Percy! Glad you could make it so fast."

Nick shook Percy's hand and motioned for him to come and sit down. Percy smiled at Harry. "Hi there. How are you doing?"

Harry got another coughing spell but when it was over, he looked at Percy. Something about Percy was forcing a part of his mind into action. *Could this guy be someone he knew?*

"Harry, you were doing a great job for me at the lumberyard. As soon as we can get the smoke damage assessed and cleaned up, you're welcome to come back to work."

A job? And I can come back to work? Is it true I have a job? Harry was doubtful, but the look on this guy's face reassured him that maybe he wasn't just feeding him a line. *I'll have to dig deeper into the blank parts of my brain and sort out some answers to those questions.*

Nick spoke up, "Harry, maybe I should take you to your place. You can get some rest and maybe your memory will come back when you see your things in your suite. I'll phone Ron to let him know we're coming."

Harry savored the last bite of biscuit and drank the remaining bit of tea. He felt better. *Guess I was hungry after all.* He pushed his chair back and nodded agreement. They walked out the door. Percy went with them and got in his car. "See you later."

Out in the car, Harry looked again at the houses on either side of Nick's place. He couldn't understand why Nick would be living in such a run-down area.

"Harry, do you remember how you got to the hospital?"

"Was I in the hospital? Maybe they gave me some drugs or somethin' that got me all mixed up. Do you think that's it?"

Harry was getting worried about this memory problem. His head didn't feel right, not dizzy, but kind of foggy, like when he drank some bad stuff on the streets. *That's it! I used to live on the streets! I remember that! But how did I get to this place?* He looked at the street signs and watched until the car stopped in front of a nice, well- kept house. He stared at it in silence.

"Are you ready to go in and check out your suite? I hope it helps jog some of those memory cells!" Nick got out of the car and walked around to the passenger side, opened the door, and helped Harry get out. "You've had a pretty tough go of it these last few hours. It's no wonder you can't remember anything. Come on, let's go in."

Harry shuffled along the sidewalk while Nick led the way and knocked on the back door. A woman about medium height, wearing a sweatshirt, and jeans opened the door.

She smiled broadly and said, "Hi, Harry! We were waiting for you! So sorry you were in that smoke-filled building. We've been praying for you. Come in."

Nick gave Harry a little nudge forward and he stepped through the open door. He looked at the kitchen area and something in his mind clicked; he had been here before! Maybe these people were telling him the truth. A tall man with a black beard and dark rimmed glasses came into the kitchen from a hallway.

"Hi, Harry. Welcome home! How are you?"

Harry kept standing in the middle of the kitchen, still trying to put things in order in his brain. Somehow, he knew this place was where he was supposed to be. He held out his hand to the young fellow and gave him a limp shake.

"My name's Ron. Do you remember me? And this is my wife, Betty. You have a suite in our basement. How about I take you down and let you look around?"

Nick nodded in agreement and watched as Ron and Harry proceeded down the stairwell.

"Betty, I'm going to go down to the hospital and see if I can get some info about what condition Harry was in when he was brought in by ambulance. Makes me wonder if they gave him drugs. Former alcoholics can't tolerate some drugs, really messes up their system."

"That's a good idea. There's definitely something wrong with him. He's not himself."

Nick buttoned up his coat and hurried out. Betty cleared the table and stacked the dishes in the sink, then went downstairs to see how Harry and Ron were doing. The door to the bedroom was slightly ajar and she could hear Ron talking quietly to Harry. In fact, it sounded like Ron was praying. She didn't want to interrupt, so went back up the stairs. As she went, she prayed aloud, "Lord Jesus, Harry is in trouble. Please help him remember where he is and who he is. Help him know that You, Lord Jesus, are here to help him through this time."

She washed the dishes and put them back in the cupboard, wiped the table and counter and sat down to wait. It felt like Ron was with Harry for a very long time. Down the stairs she went again. This time the door was still ajar, but she didn't hear any talking. She tip-toed over to the door and peered inside. She saw Harry lying on the bed fast asleep. Ron was sitting on a chair beside the bed. He motioned a "Shhh..." and indicated everything was fine. Betty waved and went back upstairs

In a few minutes, Ron came into the living room. "Phew! That was a long session, but at least he finally relaxed and went off to sleep. It seemed like he was beginning to remember some of his belongings in the room. I saw his Bible on the bedside table, so I got him to take off his jacket and shoes and lie on the bed. He seemed to be shaking a bit, so I covered him with that nice warm quilt you made, and he snuggled right down. I found the place where he had marked this morning. It was in Psalm 46, '*God is our refuge and strength, a very present help in time of trouble.*' Before I knew it, he was sound asleep. He's had a scary day. Just hope he can sleep through the night. I'll go down and check on him every couple of hours."

They heard a knock at the door. Wondering who could be there at this late hour, Ron looked through the peephole and saw Nick standing there.

"Come in!"

"You know, it's good to live in a smaller community, especially when you have connections in the right places. I went to the hospital and because I know Sherry, one of the nurses, I could get some information on what happened to Harry while he was there. When the ambulance brought him in, he was unconscious. They gave him some oxygen and he began to wake up but then he was fighting, swearing, and getting violent, so they gave him a sedative shot and cough medicine. It seemed to work at first, but when they asked him what his name was and where he lived, he was totally blank. Couldn't remember anything. About an hour after he woke up, he demanded to be let out of there, so they let him go. Sherry said the meds should wear off soon, especially if he's had something to eat and drink."

"Oh, that's good news! We'll keep a watch on him overnight. I hope he'll be better in the morning.". Ron nodded at Betty, and she agreed. "Well, Nick, you better go and get some rest yourself. Thanks for everything. Have a good night."

A few minutes later, Ron heard a loud crash in the basement.

"What the ...?" He ran down the stairs and pushed the door open to Harry's room. Harry was lying on the floor, a dazed look on his face. He wasn't moving. The bedside table was on its side and most of the blankets were rumbled up in a big pile.

"Harry! Harry! What's wrong? Are you okay?" He knelt down and checked Harry's neck pulse. He saw that he was breathing very heavily soaked in sweat. "Harry! Can you hear me?"

Harry groaned and tried to turn over. Ron pulled on his arm and helped him sit up.

"Where am I? Who are you?" Harry mumbled. He looked at Ron and then saw Betty standing in the doorway.

"Here, let me help you sit up. Betty will get you a drink of water."

Betty returned with a glass of water. Harry gulped it down and looked at the empty glass. Betty ran to get more. Harry downed that too and then leaned against the bed and took a deep breath. His eyes focused on Ron. Things began to fall into place. He looked around the room and saw his clothes, his Bible, and his shoes.

"Don' know what happened to me, but this place looks like I bin here before."

"Yes, Harry, this is your room. Are you hungry? Betty can bring you something if you'd like. How about a bologna and cheese sandwich?"

"You know, that sounds purdy good, I think I'm hungry."

Betty headed for the stairs to make the sandwich. Ron set the bedside table up and replaced the Bible and lamp. He was thankful the lamp hadn't broken when it landed on the floor. He helped Harry get up from the floor and got him to sit at the small table in the corner. Ron pulled out another chair and sat down.

"Harry do you remember me?"

Harry looked at him again and thought for a few moments. "Yeah, you're Ron. I live in your basement, right?"

"Yes! Oh, I'm so glad your memory is coming back. You scared us today when you couldn't remember who we were or what had happened to you."

Harry thought some more and then a panic expression filled his eyes. "There was a fire! I remember looking for Percy and I remember Trudy standing beside me when we got out of the building. That smoke was so thick, it got in my lungs, and I couldn't breathe, it was terrible! That's it! I remember! Except for a blank piece in the middle."

Ron nodded, "That's when you passed out. The ambulance took you to the hospital and they gave you some medicine to calm you down. It must have had a bad effect on you, like making you unable to remember anything."

Harry thought for a few more minutes, then, "What happened to Percy and Trudy? Are they okay?" His face showed a deep concern.

"They're fine, they both got out in time. In fact, the shop didn't burn down at all, just a lot of smoke damage.

They aren't sure what started it, but the firemen will figure it out.

Betty came down the stairs. "Here you are, Harry, have something to eat. She set a small tray, loaded with a hearty sandwich and a glass of milk and a cup of tea on the table.

"Thank you! I'm so thankful to have you guys take care of me." He had another coughing spell, but this time it didn't last so long. He caught his breath and took a long drink of the tea.

"Ah! That's good! I'm okay, you guys can go back up-stairs."

"Good night, Harry. Have a good sleep."

Harry looked around the room and saw the Bible on the bedside cabinet. He opened it where the bookmark was and the first verse he saw was, 'God is our refuge and strength, a very present help in time of trouble.' *Thank you, Lord, I needed that! You got me through this terrible day. Thank you for all the people that helped me and thank you that the shop didn't burn down.*

He kept reading the next verses in between eating. Each verse brought a new calmness to his heart. When he was finished, he went to the bathroom and looked at himself in the mirror. There were black smudges on his face and hands, his hair was matted, and he needed a shave. He threw off his clothes and jumped into the shower. It felt so good! He stayed there a few extra minutes, letting the water cascade down over his body. When he was done, he felt like a new man. He crawled into bed, pulled the quilt up to his chin and fell asleep.

Getting Back to Normal

HARRY WOKE TO sunshine gleaming through the basement window. He blinked and turned over. But no. He couldn't stay in bed, he had to get up and see about his job. He got dressed and hurried up the stairs. Betty was sitting in the kitchen drinking a cup of coffee and reading something on her cell phone.

"Good morning, Harry! Did you have a good rest? How about some breakfast?"

Harry pulled out a chair and sat down. "You know, that sounds like a great idea! After breakfast, I'm goin' down to the lumberyard to check it out. Have you heard anything more 'bout the fire?"

"Yes, I was just reading the latest on my phone. It says the fire started in the small kitchen. It looks like something got left in the microwave too long and when it exploded, it set some nearby papers on fire."

Harry thought about that while Betty prepared some breakfast. He thought back to yesterday morning. He had met up with Ally and took him to the cafe, then he had gone to work, but was late. He retraced his steps and then his mind froze. He remembered putting a 'go-bag' from the café in the microwave in the kitchen. Had he caused the fire? Oh no! Was he responsible? *Please, Lord, no!*

Betty placed a plate of eggs and bacon in front of Harry and poured some coffee in his cup. Harry had a hard time eating, the thought that he had caused the fire was making his stomach churn. He gathered his dishes and put them in the sink.

"Thanks for the breakfast, Betty, you're a great cook! I got to get down to the shop."

He ran to his room, grabbed his coat and cap, and rushed up the stairs. "See you later Betty." He walked the four blocks as fast as he could, even though he bent over with a coughing spell at times. At the shop, he noticed a pickup belonging to the Fire Marshal and Percy's truck sitting in the parking lot. His steps slowed, as he neared the building. *What if it was my fault? What's goin' to happen to me? Will I still have a job? What will I do?* He walked to the back of the building and opened the door with shaking hands. The two men were in deep conversation.

With great fear and trembling, he walked over to them. "Good morning. I jus' had to come by and see what happened yesterday." He was met with serious stares and silence for a few seconds.

"Harry, when you came in to work yesterday, did you see anyone else around?"

Harry looked sheepish, "No, I couldn't find Trudy or you Percy, so I set to work, piling some lumber for an order. I was kinda late, 'cause I'd taken a street guy to the café to get him some food."

The fire marshal had a questioning expression. "What was the first thing you did when you got here?"

"Ah... I...er... I had a 'go-bag' from the café with some leftover food. I put it in the microwave to warm it up."

"And then what?"

"I went to the back and got busy."

Harry started to cry. "It's all my fault ain't it? I caused the fire! I didn't mean to do it! Please believe me! I didn' mean to forget the microwave." He turned away from the men and headed for the door.

Percy ran after him, "Wait, Harry! Wait! We know it wasn't intended, it was an accident. Accidents happen. We must go on from here! Mostly, I need your help to clean up. The smoke got into everything, we need to wash things down and maybe throw some stuff out. It's a big job, but I'll keep you on if you'll help."

Harry continued to run, pushed the door open with a vicious thrust and stood outside gasping for air. "Jesus! Jesus! Help me! Please help me!" He pounded the wall with his fist, tempted to swear a blue streak, but he made a choice right there that he would not swear but instead call out to God.

"Harry, it's okay. Please, let me help you." Percy tugged on Harry's jacket and guided him by the arm. "Let's go inside and talk this over. Come on." They went back into the building and found a couple of chairs near the front entrance. The fire marshal nodded to Percy and left.

"But Percy, I made this mess! It's my fault! I can't ever do anythin' right. Seems like things always go wrong when I get in the middle. I'm gonna move on, I've done enough damage here. It's no use!"

"Harry I've been watching, noticing how you aren't like the usual street guys. You've worked hard. I saw you were faithful in your job and how you treated the people who came in for lumber. And especially how you treated Trudy with respect, even though she has a bad limp and vision problems. That goes a long way with me. You don't just think about yourself, you think of others. When I heard you saying "Jesus" out there on the doorstep, I thought you were swearing, but then - you weren't swearing were you?"

Harry sat quiet for a long time, in between coughing spells. Percy waited him out.

"You know, I'm glad you knew I wasn't swearin', that would be a slam against my Lord and Saviour. It's Jesus that brought me this far. He's brought me through a lot of tough things. Before He came into my life, I would have run for the bottle to deaden the pain or shame I was feeling. But when Jesus came and I made a choice to let Him control my life, things got a lot easier. That's not to say everythin' was all rosy and perfect, but He's been there with me through it all."

It was Percy's turn to sit quiet and think. Harry looked around and then back at Percy. *Lord, please let Percy understand what I'm sayin'.* After a long time, Harry stood up. "Well, we better get to cleaning this mess. It ain't gonna clean itself!" He walked to the back of the huge open building and searched for a bucket, mop, and rags.

They worked together in silence, except to decide what should be done next. Percy was quieter than usual and Harry just kept to himself, working as hard as he could.

At lunch time Percy called a halt. "We need to get some food. Let's go down to the café and see what they have on special today."

When they walked into the café, the first person Harry saw was Leda. His heart gave a little flip, but he lowered his eyes and followed Percy to a table by the window.

"Hi guys! I heard you've had a bad time over at the lumberyard. Is everything okay?"

Harry hung his head in shame. Percy responded quickly, "Yeah, we're trying to clean up the place. There's not much fire damage, mostly smoke. Takes a lot of work to clean it up. We've worked up an appetite. What's on special today?"

"The usual on a Friday, fish and chips, clam chowder, or hamburger deluxe, including fries. How about some coffee?" She poured coffee into the mugs that they pushed over to her.

"How about it, Harry? What'll you have?"

For some reason Harry seemed tongue-tied. "Ah, ah... I'll do the burger. Thanks," He mumbled.

"I'll try your chowder and the fish, sounds good!"

Leda hurried away to place the order. They drank their coffee in silence, until Leda brought their orders.

"Looks great! Your chef knows how to put food together! Thank you!"

Percy was about to dig into the chowder when Harry raised his eyes and said, "Can I ask a blessing on the food before we eat?"

Percy dropped his spoon with a clang and bowed his head. Harry prayed a simple prayer, thanking God for His care, for the food, and for Percy. Harry opened his eyes and saw that Percy was looking very sober. Harry began to munch on the fries and looked the burger over. It was huge! There were layers of lettuce, tomato, pickles, cheese, and a very large hamburger patty. With difficulty he got his mouth around it for the first bite. All he could say was "Mm...!" Percy nodded in agreement as he finished the last of the soup and dug into the fish and chips.

Leda came over "How's your meal, guys? Jody is a good chef, right?"

They both nodded to her but kept on eating. Harry seemed so engrossed in his food that it looked like he didn't care what she said. But in his mind, he kept thinking, *She's the most beautiful woman I've ever set eyes on. I don' know how to handle these feelings. She sure wouldn't want anythin' to do with the likes of me!*

When they were finished, Percy went over to pay the bill and Harry got busy putting his jacket on. Leda waved good-bye to them, and Harry kind of raised his hand, acknowledging her wave. At the yard they got back to work, and within a couple of hours they had made real progress.

"Well, that's enough for today. I'm tired! You must be tired too."

"Yeah, it's been a bumpy couple of days. I ain't as young as I used to be!"

They put their equipment away and Percy locked the doors.

On the way home, Harry had to go by the café. He wondered if Leda was still there or was off shift. He didn't have the nerve to go in and check. A few steps down the block, he spied Ally. He was sitting on a bench near the liquor store, a bottle in his hand. Harry forgot about Leda and focused on Ally.

"Hey, Ally! How are you doin'? I missed seein' you yesterday. Been kinda busy – what with the fire and all."

"I thought I heard some noise the other day, but didn' pay much 'tention."

"Yeah, there was a fire at the lumberyard where I work, mostly smoke damage. We've been cleanin' it up all day. Have you had anything to eat today?"

"Yeah, some guys came along handing out sandwiches an' water. Don't know who they were, but they seemed friendly enough. I'll be fine."

Harry decided he better get home; Betty would have supper ready. "See you 'round, Ally."

Back at the house, Harry went down to his suite to get cleaned up. The aroma of something delicious wafted down the stairs and his stomach growled.

During the meal, Harry decided he needed to tell them about the fire.

"Betty, remember what you said this morning about the fire?"

Betty nodded.

"Well the fire was my fault." He went on to explain about the 'go-bag'

"Oh Harry! I'm sorry." Betty reached across the table and patted his arm.

"I'm so thankful that Percy let me stay. He coulda fired me on the spot, but he didn't. I worked with him all day, helpin' to clean up the mess."

"Percy is a good guy." Ron asserted.

Conversation turned to the happenings of their day. Ron mentioned something about a group from their church going out and handing out food to the street people.

Harry's ears perked up. "I stopped and talked to Ally on the way home and he told me about some guys handing out sandwiches."

"That would be Larry and Ben, their wives make the sandwiches in the church kitchen and then take them around. They hope to show the street people that there really are some people that care about them."

Harry nodded and wiped his mouth, "That was a great meal, Betty! I was getting very hungry. All that scrubbing and sorting was hard work, I'm beat! Gonna head for the 'hay'. Thanks, and good night."

"Good night, Harry, have a good sleep."

Just before crawling into bed, Harry opened his Bible. Things had been all mixed up. He noticed a passage was marked at John chapter 10. He read the verse that had a big star near it. It was verse 14 *"I am the good Shepherd, my sheep know my voice and follow me."*

"Thank you, Lord, for your help today and your help through the fire and that it wasn't any worse. Thank you that I could share you with Percy and Ally. Help me to live the life you want me to live. Good night, Lord".

Another Hospital Visit

THE NEXT MORNING, he was up early to read his Bible and pray. At breakfast he asked Betty if she'd pray that he would be able to share Jesus with whoever came across his path that day. She gladly agreed and prayed a short blessing on him before he headed out the door with his lunch bag. At the lumberyard he found Percy hard at work.

"Good mornin', you beat me here! I did't think you'd be here so early!"

"Had to get going on this job. Customers are coming in later and we need to be ready to fill their orders. Can you go in the back and load up a few pallets for old Archie that lives across the other side of town? He phoned and ordered them before the fire and he's anxious to pick them up."

"Sure 'nough. I'll get right at it."

Harry hurried to get the job done. He had caused enough trouble and didn't want Percy to lose a customer because of him. When he was done, he went back inside, picked up a bucket and some rags and went to help. Before he knew it the clock said it was already after lunch. He retrieved his lunch bag from the fridge and sat down to eat. Percy had said he would be back in a half hour, so Harry had time alone to pray and to think about the verse he read in the Bible. He didn't know much about sheep, but he'd heard that sheep were kind of hard to care for. He'd also heard that they like to wander away from the shepherd and go their own way. He could understand how people could be compared to sheep. He knew in himself that he could get side- tracked so easily and forget to keep his eyes on Jesus. He decided to be extra careful to live joyfully, to be kind, and show the love of Jesus to those who weren't that easy to love. He prayed a short prayer and then went back to work.

By the end of the day, they had got about half of the supplies cleaned up. In the middle, Archie came for his order and they had to stop and visit with him and tell him about the fire. While they were talking, a farmer came in. He looked around at the mess and was about to walk out, when Percy called to him.

"Hey, Tommy! Sorry the place is kind of upside down, but we're still open for business. Can I get something for you?"

"Oh, I didn't think you were open. Sorry about the fire. Looks like you're getting it all back in order."

"Yes, Harry has been helping me a lot. What can we get for you?"

Tommy pulled out a list from his pocket and showed it to Percy. Percy handed it to Harry and nodded for him to go ahead and fill the order. Harry loaded the forklift and drove it to the large loading door. He went back inside and told the guys it was ready. It was then that Trudy came in through the front door. She apologized for being late but rushed to the office to get the computer up and running so she could process the order. Soon she came out with the invoice and handed it to Percy. He looked it over and handed it to Tommy.

"Looks like everything is in order," Tommy said.

"Okay. Harry, go and load his truck up. Thanks for coming in Tommy. See you around."

Harry came back into the front part of the business, ready to get back to work. Percy looked at him rather strangely. *Oh, oh, looks like I've done something wrong again.* Harry went over the work he had just completed, trying to think if he had made a mistake.

"Harry, you've been working real hard and that cough seems to be getting worse. Maybe you better go back to the doctor. You might need some medicine to get that stuff out of your lungs."

Harry felt a surge of anger rising. "I don't need a doctor!" Just the mention of a doctor set him on edge. He made a lame apology and agreed he needed some rest.

"I'll go home and have a sleep, then I'll be fine. You don't need to worry 'bout me."

Percy still had that strange look on his face, but Harry ignored it, got his jacket and left.

Back at the house he noticed that neither Ron nor Betty were around, but that didn't bother him. He went straight to his room, closed the door and sank down on his bed. He couldn't understand why he was so tired; he hadn't been working that hard. Before he knew it, he was asleep.

   ***

Betty was busy making supper when Ron came home. "Have you seen Harry? I've been away all day. Don't know if he's going to be here for supper."

Ron replied, "Nope, haven't seen or heard anything about him at all."

They waited for a while, but then decided to eat, Harry would show up when he was ready. The evening was quiet, but Ron got to wondering about Harry. It was already past eight o'clock. Something told him he should go down and see if Harry was in his room.

Ron knocked on Harry's door. No answer. He knocked again. He tried the knob and slowly opened the door. In the dim light he saw Harry lying on the bed.

"Harry! Harry!" No answer. He shook Harry's shoulder. No response. "Betty! Come down here! Hurry!"

Betty ran into the room and took one look at Harry. Something was very wrong with him. "I'll call 911!"

The EMS staff did an assessment and determined his blood sugar levels and blood pressure were very high. They made the decision to take him to the hospital.

Bad News

"SIR! HARRY! CAN you hear me?"

A nurse was standing over the stretcher, gently shaking his shoulder.

Harry slowly became aware of his surroundings. He looked at the ceiling and knew he wasn't in his suite. He noticed the curtain pulled around the stretcher and it dawned on him that he was in the hospital – again! He panicked. He was so afraid of hospitals, he had bad memories of them from when he was a kid. Every time he was in one, something bad happened. The memories flooded back.

"Help! Help!" He yelled.

"Please, sir! You need to rest. Just rest, we're trying to help you." The ER doctor came in with the results of the blood tests that were done when Harry arrived. He ordered an IV, oxygen, and some insulin.

Harry was so weak he had no choice but to obey what the nurse said. He lay back on the pillow and went back to sleep.

"How is he doing?" Ron and Betty were at the Nursing Station.

"Are you family?" the nurse wanted to know.

"He doesn't have any family that we know of. He lives in our basement suite."

"He was awake for a short time but is sleeping now. Maybe wait for about fifteen minutes."

They went back to the waiting area and made a call to Pastor Nick. They explained the situation as best they could and asked if he could come.

The nurse came into the waiting area and said, "You can come and see him now; he's awake."

"What are you guys doin' here? How come I'm here?" Harry struggled to sit up.

"No, Harry, you don't have to sit up. We're here because you're very sick. We found you unconscious in your bed. We had to call the ambulance."

Harry tried to make sense of what they were saying. He didn't remember being sick.

"You're just trying to make up a story so you could get me back in the hospital. I want outta here!" He made another attempt to sit up.

The nurse came in and talked gently to him, and he relaxed. Ron laid a hand on Harry's arm, "Harry, we've called Pastor Nick, he'll be here soon. Then we can pray with you."

Harry gave a short nod and turned his head to the wall. The IV tubing got in his way. He was getting tangled up in it and was about to yank at it, but Betty saw what was going to happen and ran to the other side of the stretcher.

"It's okay, Harry, the IV is going to help you feel better. Don't pull on it, just rest."

Pastor Nick appeared at the foot of the stretcher, and then went to the side so Harry could see him. Betty stepped back.

"Harry, it's me, Pastor Nick."

Harry opened his eyes and gaped at the pastor. *Am I that sick that they've called the pastor to give me 'last rites'?* Fear gripped his stomach again.

"Harry, let me read you something from Psalms 46, maybe it will help you rest. *'God is our refuge and strength, a very present help in time of trouble.'*. Harry, Jesus is here with you right now, He won't leave you. He has promised to be with you wherever you are. He knows your fears and He cares about every part of you, and your life."

Harry relaxed and took the words in. *Yes, Lord, you ARE with me. Thank you, I need that promise.*

"Harry, do you want me to read some more?"

"Yes, please, that really helps."

Ron and Betty motioned to the pastor that they were going to leave, and Nick indicated he would stay. Then he quietly read more from some other Psalms.

Harry began to relax more. The fear in his belly was going away. "What do you suppose is wrong with me? Nobody is telling me anything. I'm scared of hospitals," he admitted.

"Harry, the doctors and nurses are here to help you, not to hurt you. I don't know what's wrong, but I'll see if I can get some information." He made his way out to the Nursing Station.

Pastor Nick came back into the room with a nurse close behind. "Harry, this is Julia, she's going to tell you what's happened, and why you're here. She can do it better than I can."

Julia came to the other side of the stretcher and put her hand on the side rail.

"Harry, your friend tells me you don't know why you're here or what's wrong. We've done some tests and the results are back. Your blood sugar levels were really high. The normal is around five, yours was 24!" She stopped talking and waited for that news to register with Harry.

"You mean that's why I passed out?"

"Yes, when your sugar levels get too high, they can do bad things in your body. Do you know what that means?"

"Not really." Harry turned his head away from the nurse. *I'm lyin', I know what it means. It means I've got Diabetes. No! Lord! I can't have Diabetes! I know what happens when you have Diabetes – really bad things, and then you die!*

"Harry, please listen to me."

But Harry kept his face turned away from her. He looked up at the pastor in desperation, "Pastor Nick, can you help me? Please!"

"I'm here, Harry. Let the nurse finish what she was saying."

"I was lying, I know what high sugar levels mean. I've got Diabetes, right?"

Julia nodded but didn't say anything for a few minutes. Then, "How much do you know about Diabetes, Harry?"

"Too much! My late Mom and Auntie both died from it. I don' wanna die!"

"Harry, sometimes a big stressful time – like the fire at your work, can set off the tendency you might have to get Diabetes. It doesn't mean you're going to die. We can help you learn how to live with it. We have people who are trained to teach you."

Harry looked at her, his eyes full of doubt, he didn't believe her. *You don' live with Diabetes, you die with it! It's gonna take a lot of convincing from this little lady before I'll even begin to believe her.*

Learning a New Routine

THE NEXT DAY the nurse and dietician began talking to Harry about how to live with Diabetes. They gave him a bunch of papers and talked so much his brain couldn't take it in. Later in the day, the doctor came in and told him he could go home. The nurse said they would call his friend Ron to come and get him.

Back at his suite, he sat on the bed in deep thought, trying to sort through all that had happened in the last few days. It had only been four days, but it felt like a year! He looked at the bag full of booklets and papers. *How am I supposed to get all that stuff figured out?*

Sunday came, and he looked forward to going to church. He needed some spiritual support more than anything. Ron and Betty gave him a ride. They walked into the foyer and were welcomed by several people. Some spoke to Harry, telling him they had been praying for him when they heard about the fire, and of him being in hospital. That made him feel better. These people cared about what happened to him!

The service began with a worship time of singing and praising God for who He is and for all He has done for us. Harry couldn't sing very well, but that didn't matter, he croaked along with the rest of the congregation, just thankful he was alive and could even be at church. After the singing was over, people took a few minutes to say hello to each other.

It was during this time that Leda suddenly appeared in front of him. She put her hand on his arm and said, "Harry, I'm sorry about all your troubles. I've been praying for you."

Harry was speechless. All he could do was nod a 'thank you' before Pastor Nick announced he was about to begin the sermon. Leda returned to her seat, but Harry didn't miss seeing where she was sitting a couple of rows ahead on the other side of the sanctuary. Her light brown hair glistened in the light. Again he thought he'd never seen anything quite so beautiful! He tried to concentrate on the sermon, but his eyes kept wandering over to the other side of the building. In between, he heard Pastor Nick talking about how Job, in the Bible, went through many losses and troubles, but that he never stopped trusting God.

"When God tests us and allows things to go wrong, we know that God is always there. He never leaves us. We know that because He promised it in His Word, *'I will never leave you, nor forsake you. '* If anyone wants to come up for prayer, please come and see me after I close the service. Let's pray."

Harry knew he should go up for prayer, but he was torn between tracking Leda down and obeying the urging of the Holy Spirit. He decided he better obey. God would work it out for him to see Leda. After the prayer time, he felt much better, like he could face the future, knowing Jesus was with him all the way. He had known that ever since he had let Jesus come into his life, but sometimes he forgot.

Ron and Betty were visiting with friends in the foyer, when he came out of the sanctuary. He stood there until they were ready to go.

"Harry, we'd like to take you out for lunch. How about it?"

Harry's mind immediately froze. *What 'bout my Diabetes? How am I supposed to eat in a restaurant?* He felt panic coming on. He was scared to eat because he didn't want to end up in the hospital again. "Naw, I think I'd rather just go home, thanks just the same."

"Harry, I can help you choose the best things on the menu. You have to eat! Starving yourself won't work. I looked over some of the papers you got from the hospital." Harry looked at her, still not believing that he could go and eat in a restaurant without getting sick.

Betty motioned for him to follow. "Let's go and give it a try

With Betty's help, Harry enjoyed the delicious meal, and had to admit he felt better afterwards. He was beginning to understand that being a Diabetic wasn't a death sentence. Maybe he would survive.

"But It's So Hard!"

BACK AT WORK on Monday, Percy was in a positive mood. "Good morning Harry! Things are looking good. We're almost finished the clean up so we can get back to serving our customers."

They set to work on the last section of the storage area and were pleased with themselves when they saw it was done. They stopped for a rest and Harry remembered Betty had made him a small lunch to be eaten mid-morning. He wasn't hungry, but decided he'd better eat anyway.

Percy sat and drank his coffee, smoking a cigarette. The aroma of smoke triggered memories in Harry's mind of days gone by. Like how he would sit with his family when he was little and the elders would tell stories and jokes, making everyone laugh. He missed those days. He had gone through so much since then. Like living on the streets for years, working on the farm that belonged to Dave and Mable, and then for JayJay. But before that, he remembered being at the homeless shelter and how Leo and his friends had told him about Jesus. Then the peace he had felt in his whole being when he finally admitted he couldn't get his life sorted out on his own, and that he needed Jesus' help. Life had not been all roses and comfort, yet he knew he was loved by God. His deep thought was abruptly interrupted by Percy.

"Hey, Harry! Are you okay? Seemed liked you weren't here for a while."

"Oh, sorry. The cigarette smoke reminded me of when I was a little kid, and then my mind went tearing along over the years. Didn't mean to ignore you. Well, better get back to work."

At the end of the day, Harry surveyed the huge piles of lumber in the storage area. He was mighty pleased. Life was getting back to normal.

"See you, Percy. I'll be heading home now." Harry waved and walked out the door. Percy nodded and locked the doors.

On his way home, he looked in the window of the café, hoping to see if Leda was there, but the windows were kind of dirty and he couldn't see in. He looked for Ally too, but he was nowhere to be found.

At home, Betty greeted him warmly. "I've been reading all those papers that you got from the hospital. I've tried a new recipe from them. Hope you like it."

At supper, they discussed their day and also how finding out you are a Diabetic is a life-changing experience. Harry admitted he was scared of all the things he was required to do, like check his sugar levels and to eat on a regular basis. He had never eaten on a regular basis most of his life.

"We're here to help you, Harry. It's just like when you decided to follow Jesus. You made a choice for the better way of living. This is the same. God has given us only one body, and He wants us to take care of it by eating right, by staying close to Him, and by reading His Word and obeying it."

"Guess you're right, but it don't happen all at once. I learned that a long time ago." He excused himself from the table and went to his room. He felt so tired. He decided to lay down for a few minutes before he got ready for bed.

    ***

"Harry! Are you getting up? It's breakfast time!" Betty was knocking on the door, sounding rather concerned.

Harry moaned and rolled over. He was having such a good sleep and having an amazing dream. "Huh? Oh! I'm getting up. Thanks." He looked at his rumbled clothes and saw that he had slept in them all night. He must have been really tired! He jumped in the shower, got dressed, and hurried up the stairs.

"Sorry! I didn' mean to miss breakfast! Don't know why I was so tired. Fell asleep right after supper."

"Harry, did you take your pills yesterday? The ones to keep your sugar down?"

Harry was hung his head, "Ah, no. I think I forgot. I'm not used to taking pills." He ran down to his room and went through his dirty clothes. There, deep in his pants pocket, he found the little pill box Betty had given him.

Back at the table he put the pills beside his plate and waited until Ron said the blessing. In the prayer, Ron asked the Lord to help Harry remember to take his pills and to eat his snacks and lunch.

"How are you doing with checking your sugar?" Betty questioned.

Harry was embarrassed again and had to admit he hadn't tried it at all. *Wonder if she's ever tried poking her finger with a needle? It hurts!*

"Do you want me to help you, Harry?"

"Yeah, guess I need some help. It's pretty scary."

Together they read over the instructions and managed to get some blood on the little test strip. The reading said '12.8'!

"Oh my, Harry that's not good. No wonder you were so tired. With the Lord's help, you can do better, I'm sure!"

All through the week, Harry tried and tried to follow all the rules about eating, taking his pills and checking his sugar. In a few days he was getting a little more accustomed to poking his finger and decided it wasn't so bad after all. Each day he prayed that he would obey the rules and obey God's Word.

Saturday morning, he slept in a bit. When he got up, he realized it wasn't an effort to crawl out of bed like it had been. *Maybe this diet and pills idea is better than the way it was before. It's hard, but I'll keep trying.*

He was looking forward to Sunday again. He loved the music and maybe, just maybe, he might get a glimpse of Leda! He sternly told himself, *don't get yourself all excited about that woman! She don' want nothin' to do with you. She's too classy for you. Just keep your mind on your work and your new routine.*

At church, a few people said hello and then mingled with their own group of friends. Harry felt rather left out. He didn't have anybody to talk to. He knew most of the people had known each other for years and that he was a newcomer. In a couple of other churches, he had attended after coming to know Jesus, he had found there were little cliques of friends who tended to gather in their own corners. He had been thankful for those who had taken the extra time to include him in their group, but this church was different. Maybe because there were no other Indigenous people there, they didn't know how to interact with him. Ron tried to include Harry in his group, but the other men looked uncomfortable, in fact, they looked downright irritated, like 'you don't belong here'.

Harry heard the music begin and went into the sanctuary. He sat in the same place as before and soon found his gaze wandering over to the other side of the room. *There she is!* His heart flip- flopped. He saw her talking to some other ladies, waving her hands and laughing. *Man! Would I ever love to know what she's talkin' about. She looks so lively. Lord, could you please let me talk to her sometime? Oh, sorry, I'm trying to follow your lead. I'll let you bring a meeting with her if and when it's your time.*

Pastor Nick spoke about listening to God's voice, and that the only way to hear His voice was to stay in the Word. To keep reading, and seeking, and asking the Lord for His will and way in our lives. Harry nodded every once in a while, in agreement. He knew what he needed to do, the problem was to stick with it and do it!

After the service, Leda seemed to disappear into the crowd and Harry moved on, joining Ron and Betty in the car on the way home. At the dinner table they talked about the sermon.

"I'm finding it really hard to keep obeying the Lord." Ron admitted.

Harry was surprised. *He's been a Christian for a long time. Thought he had it all together. Don't it get easier?*

Betty agreed. "It's not easy, is it? What about you Harry, how's it going for you?"

Harry was quiet for a long time, and they ate in silence. "I thought it gets easier when you've been following the Lord for a long time. Don't it?"

Ron shook his head. "No, Harry, it doesn't get easier. Satan doesn't want us to follow the Lord, he wants us to go back to the old ways. You know what a mess that was. We must keep working at following the Lord. The Bible says in 1 Peter, 'work at your salvation' – we have to put some effort into it too, not just sit back and wait for the Lord to make all the moves."

Break In!

THE WEEK DAWNED bright and sunny, and Harry was eager to get to work. He walked with his head held high. It was going to be a good day! *Thank you, Lord, for this day You have made. Thank you for my job and thank you for Ron and Betty.*

When he arrived at the lumberyard, he couldn't see Percy's truck anywhere and Trudy's bike wasn't in the bike rack either. He looked at his watch, it was 8:30 am. Percy was always there early to open up and get things ready for the day. He walked around to the back of the building and then to the front again, still no Percy. He looked down the street, hoping Percy would be coming. Nothing. *Please Jesus! Help me! I don't know what to do!* He went to the back again and stood there a few more minutes, resisting the temptation to try the door, then turned and walked back down the street.

I'll just go into the café and see if anyone shows up. Inside the café he saw the same group of guys that had been there the day he brought Ally in for a sandwich. Some of them ignored him, but one guy made a rude remark. Harry paid no attention.

He sat down at a table as far away as he could from the group. An older lady came out of the back and offered him a coffee. He was too shy to ask if Leda was working, so he drank his coffee. He looked out the window every once in a while to see if Percy's truck might be going by, but nothing. He paid for his coffee and walked back to the lumberyard. On the way, he stopped at a drugstore and asked the clerk if she had seen Percy around. She shrugged and indicated she didn't know and didn't care.

By now it was nearly 9:30, this was very strange. Just as he was deciding to walk back home, he saw Percy's truck roaring up to the property in a cloud of dust. Percy jumped out of the truck and ran to the back door. Harry hurried and went around the building. The door was hanging open and he heard Percy swearing and yelling inside. Harry cautiously entered through the door. It was then he saw a huge mess. Lumber and supplies were strewn all over the floor, some racks were broken, and a few lights smashed.

"Percy! What happened?" Harry yelled. Percy stopped long enough to glower at Harry, then he let out a torrent of cussing and swearing.

"You .... Indian! It's all your fault. I never should have trusted you! You're nothing but trouble, you're fired!!"

Harry stood there with his mouth open, hands held out in surrender. Percy was so mad he wouldn't even let Harry say anything. No one had been this angry with him for a long time. He turned and ran out the door. *Lord, help! You know I didn' go in there. You know it ain't my fault.* He retraced the path home, tears threatening to spill over as he almost ran down the sidewalk.

"Harry! How come you're home?" Betty took one look and asked, "What happened?" Harry's face was red, his eyes flashing, as he jammed his hands into his pockets and then pulled them out.

"Somebody broke into the lumberyard and made a big mess. They broke stuff and spread it all over. Percy thinks I did it. He fired me!"

"Oh no! I don't believe he would do that. Are you sure?"

"Yes, he was so mad he was swearin' and cussin' and calling me a no-good Indian and that I've caused him nothing but trouble."

"But that's not true! You've been a good worker and he was pleased with your work."

"Yes, but I was the one that caused the fire, so he jumped to conclusions and figured I'd done the break-in too. What am I going to do? It's hard to find a job in this town, maybe I should just move on."

Betty handed him a fresh cup of coffee and a small sandwich. "Here, sit down and rest a minute, I'm going to call Pastor Nick. We need some help in this situation."

She went into the small den off the kitchen. Harry could hear her talking but she was talking low and he didn't catch everything. Betty came back into the kitchen with a Bible in her hand.

"Harry, Jesus told us, '...in this world you will have troubles. But be of good cheer I have overcome the world...' John 16:33. Do you remember what we were talking about yesterday after church? That things aren't always easy, just because we follow the Lord."

Harry nodded but kept his head down. *It's fine for her to talk about these things, she ain't homeless and jobless.*

She kept on talking, but Harry wasn't listening much. He was trying to think of a way out. He'd been in bad places before and sometimes the bottle was his only refuge. When he had it in his hand, he felt strong and forgot about his troubles. But it was like the Lord reminded him about how he felt after the bottle was empty. *Yeah, I know, I know! I didn' feel better after the booze wore off. In fact, I felt worse, so then I'd look for another one.*

"Harry, are you listening to me?" Betty lowered her head so she could see his eyes. He finally lifted his head.

"Oh, Harry, forgive me. I've rattled on not even giving you a chance to say anything. I'll shut-up and listen for a change, I'm always so ready to give advice and to natter on about stuff that doesn't matter. Please, I'll be quiet." She sat down across from him.

"You know, Betty, I ain't bin a Christian for very long. I know that the Lord is with me all the time, but when things get rocky, the first thing I want is a bottle of booze. I don't want it, but it rears its ugly head and wants to pull me back down into that hole again. I ain't strong enough to resist it sometimes." He hung his head and let the tears fall. Betty handed him a tissue.

"I can't stay here, I don't have a job, I can't pay my room and board. I'm done!" He pushed the chair back from the table, his coffee and food untouched.

"Harry! Please! You don't have to leave! I'll talk to Ron. We'll help you find another job. We like having you here." Betty sat facing Harry, tears filling her own eyes as she pleaded with him.

"I'm going down to my room and think this over. My head's in a big jumble."

"Harry, please take this food with you, remember you need to have something to eat to go with the pills you're taking."

"That's another thing. I don't want any food and I don't want you telling me what to do and when to do it! I ain't got Diabetes, I ain't sick. You're the one that's sick!"

He stomped down the stairs went into his room and slammed the door. He flopped down on the bed, covered his head with his pillow, and moaned. The world was up-side down. He couldn't think right. He felt bad that he had yelled at Betty. He knew she was trying to help him, but he couldn't stand any more. Things had been going along so good. Why did Percy yell at him; he hadn't done anything. He thought back over the events of the morning, about the door at the back of the lumberyard. Something had kept him from touching that door handle. It was like a hand had held him back. Harry was glad his fingerprints weren't on it. He heard someone pounding on the door. He tried to ignore it, but whoever it was kept on.

"What do you want?" He yelled from under his pillow.

"Harry! Harry! The cops are here. They want to talk to you." Betty's voice was insistent.

Harry threw the pillow on the floor and sat on the side of the bed. His reflection in the mirror across the room revealed rumpled clothing and mussed up hair. He went over to the dresser and brushed his hair, went into the bathroom, and splashed some water on his face.

"Harry! Are you awake?" Betty's voice was more urgent than before. Harry strode to the door and pulled it open. Betty was standing there with a cop who was glaring at him.

"Are you Harry Bearpaw?" the cop demanded in a threatening manner.

"Yeah, that's me." Harry had met many cops over the years, some were mean, others, not so much. He felt that this one was a mean one by the way he asked the question. *No point getting' him more ruffled. He knew how to handle that kind.*

"Excuse me sir, can you tell me why you're here?"

The cop scowled, "You know very well why I'm here. You know all about the break-in at the lumberyard!"

Harry made an attempt to protest that statement, but the cop interrupted.

"Come with me! We're going to the station. Hurry it up, I haven't got all day!"

Harry motioned with up-turned hands while Betty shrugged. Harry grabbed his jacket and led the way up the stairs. At the station he was pushed down the hall to a small room.

"We're going to take your fingerprints. I'll bet they match the ones at the yard. You no good Indian!"

When the task was done, they showed Harry to another room and told him to wait there. *"Well, Lord, it's been a long time since I was in one of these places. You know that I ain't done nothin' wrong.* He sat and waited in silence. He looked at his watch and saw that it was well past one o'clock, his stomach was rumbling, and he didn't feel good at all. He felt a surge of anger rising from deep inside, anger like he hadn't felt for a long time. *It's not fair! Just because of the colour of my skin they automatically decide I done somethin' wrong.* It wasn't the first time that had happened, but back before he had changed his life around, he would fight tooth and nail to defend his innocence. Now, he wasn't sure how to handle it. Things he had read in the Bible came to his mind. 'Turn the other cheek'; 'love your enemies'; 'do good to all men'. *Yeah, that's easy when things are goin' along fine, it's a lot different when things are goin' all wrong.* Harry waited and waited, in the meantime, the anger subsided, and he awaited his fate.

A different cop came in and sat down across from Harry. "Tell me what happened this morning." He was at least civil and talked in a pleasant manner.

Harry looked at him again, checking to see if he could trust this guy. He lowered his eyes and began his side of the story.

"I was goin' to work as usual, enjoying the walk, thankin' the Lord for a new day. When I got to the lumber yard, I didn't see Percy's truck, so I went around to the back. I thought about goin' in, but something kept me from trying the door handle. I decided to go over to the café and have a coffee to wait and see if Percy showed up. On my way back, Percy's truck flew by. I hurried and got there after he had gone in the building. That's when I saw the big mess."

"I see." The officer stood up and walked out of the room.

Harry tried to sort out the happenings of the morning. The first cop came back along with the second one. The second one sat down across from Harry, while the other one stood by the door with his arms crossed.

"Harry, we've checked your fingerprints against the ones on the door handle." Harry held his breath. "There are prints there, but they aren't yours."

Harry hung his head. *Thank you, Lord!*

"However, because of the recent fire and all the troubles that's been going on at the lumberyard, Percy still wants to lay charges. You'll have to post bail."

Harry looked up, eyes wide, questions on raised eyebrows. "Excuse me sir, but charges for what? Bail? I don't have any money."

"Something about you setting the fire on purpose and wanting to shut his business down." Harry sat in silence for a long time. "Can I call my pastor, please?"

"I suppose. Who is it?" The cop looked quite skeptical.

"It's Pastor Nick Redding over at the Community Church." Harry waited.

"Usually, people want to talk their lawyer, not a pastor, but okay, I'll get him on the phone for you." Both men left the room.

Please, Lord. Help me! Here I am, in a big mess again. Why is this happenin' to me? Why have you gone an' left me?

The nice cop came back with a portable phone and handed it to Harry.

"Hello? Pastor Nick? I'm in big trouble. Can you come and see me, please!" He listened intently, nodding his head in understanding. "Okay, thanks." He handed the phone back to the cop. "He can't come today, he's off on business over in Smithville. He won't be back till late tonight."

"Is there anyone else you can call?" The man looked quite sympathetic.

"Maybe call my landlord. Maybe he can give me a ride home." He gave the number and watched him dial and hand him the phone. It rang and rang then went to the voice mail.

"Ron, it's me, Harry. Can you come and get me from the 'cop shop'?" He hit the 'end' button and gave the phone back. "Guess, I'll have to walk back home, nobody around."

"Uh, we can't just let you walk out. Charges have been laid against you. Guess you didn't hear what I said. You have to post bail before you can leave." The cop uttered his words almost in an apologetic manner.

"Bail!!" Harry felt the anger again. *How was he supposed to make bail? Percy hadn't paid him, and his bank account barely had enough in it to last till the end of the month.* He fought the feeling but it kept threatening to spill over. He clenched his hands and pounded his fists on his leg.

"Leave me alone!" The cop retreated from the room and closed the door quietly.

The hours went by at a snail's pace. Harry counted the tiles in the ceiling, then he counted the tiles on the floor. Eventually the nice cop came back with a coffee and a sandwich.

"Thought you might be getting hungry." He put the tray down on the table and was about to turn and leave when Harry cleared his throat.

"Has my landlord called?"

"No. No one has called. Sorry." And left.

The hopelessness of the situation loomed in Harry's mind. There was nothing to do but pray. For the next while he sat and prayed quietly. *Lord, you know where I am. You know everythin' about me. You know me inside and out. I don't know how or what to pray. You have to take over here, I'm done.*

He put the chair up against the wall, leaned his head back and shut his eyes. He was tired. Very tired. The sandwich had helped a bit and the coffee had tasted good, but it didn't fix his dilemma, he was still confined to this windowless, bare room. By four o'clock, he looked at his watch for the umpteenth time and shook his head. *Had they forgotten about him? When were they going to let him out of here? At least they could put him in a cell while they decided what to do with him.*

He heard the doorknob turning and glanced up. He was surprised to see Betty standing there with the nice cop.

"Harry! I just got your message a few minutes ago, I was out all day and Ron is at work." She turned to the policeman.

"Constable Riley, let me talk to Harry alone, please."

The cop closed the door behind her and left.

"Harry, what happened? Tell me."

Harry told her he didn't know how he was going to get out of this place, because he didn't have money for bail. He dropped his head on his chest, covered his head with his hands, and let out a big sigh.

"Okay, Harry. I'm going to go and talk to the Constable again and see what has to be done to get you out of here. I'll be back." She went to open the door but found it locked. She knocked several times, attempting to get someone's attention. Presently, the door opened. This time the nice cop was nowhere to be seen; it was the mean one that stood there scowling.

"So, are you scared to be in here with this creep? Guess I'll let you out for now." He motioned for Betty to exit. As soon as she was out, he slammed the door real hard.

Again, Harry sat and waited and kept on praying. *I trust you Lord, no matter what happens. You brought me out of lots of scrapes before. I'm trustin' you.*

The next time Betty came into the room, Ron was with her. "Harry, we've talked to the Constable and sorted out what the charges are. Percy claims the fire in the lumber-yard was done by an arsonist, and that you were that person. The bail is posted at $300.00. We've paid it for now so you can come home with us."

"But how can you do that, and why would you do that? I'm not worth it. I told you, I can't pay rent now that I don' have a job. Just leave me here."

"No, Harry, we won't leave you here. You're coming home with us. Come on." Ron put his hand on Harry's arm and urged him to go with them. Harry decided he didn't have any other option.

At the house, he wasn't sure what to do. Should he go down to his room or just sit in the kitchen and wait for supper?

"Harry, sit here while I get supper made. Have some tea. You've had a rough day." She set a mug down in front of him. "By the way, did you take your pills today?"

Harry felt his jacket pocket, then his pants. "Oh, here they are. I forgot to take them this morning, there was too much going on." He took a pill out of the bottle and downed it with the tea.

Before they began to eat, Ron prayed a long prayer. "Lord, thank you for your everlasting love, care, and faith-fulness to us and especially, to Harry. You know all the happenings of this day and Lord, you know that Harry is innocent. Please give us direction and help us to figure out how to get this straightened out. We need You right now, more than ever before. You have promised to be our helper and our protector. We trust you to do things accord-ing to your will and way. Bless this food, we thank you for it. Amen." They ate in silence for several minutes. Harry didn't know what to say until he was almost finished.

"Thank you, Betty, that food was great! I feel a whole lot better now. Maybe I can think straight. Why do you suppose Percy got so riled up? He was treating me real good and seemed to be glad for my help to clean up the place after the fire. I wonder what set him off?"

Ron and Betty nodded in agreement but didn't have an answer either. The phone rang in the office off the kitchen. Ron went to answer it. "Yes, Harry is here. Yes, come on over." He came back to the kitchen. "Pastor Nick is on his way. He wasn't sure where you were." Betty cleared the table, just before the pastor arrived.

"Hello Harry, sorry I was out of town today and couldn't come when you called. Tell me what's going on." He shook Harry's hand and sat down. Harry went over the long story. He was getting awfully tired of trying to defend himself. He was innocent and that was all that mattered.

"I see." Pastor Nick nodded. He sat there for a while. "Harry, you know there are some people who hate Indigenous people. They'll do everything in their power to make things go bad in the hope that the person will leave. They think only 'good, white people' should live here. I'm not sure where that idea came from, but it's a fact of life. I'm sorry, but that's the way it is. I suspect they saw an opportunity to run you out of town when there was a fire and a break-in, so they got a hold of Percy and fed him a bunch of lies."

Betty chimed in. "Yes, that's probably right. The Constable at the police station said the fingerprints on the backdoor handle weren't Harry's, and it was the same on the inside where tables and other stuff had been strewn around."

Pastor Nick continued, "I'm going to call a special emergency prayer meeting tonight. This situation needs prayer! I've sent out a message to my prayer warriors and most of them are able to come. I believe God is going to bring something good out of this mess, Harry. Nothing is impossible with God!" He shook Harry's hand, put on his coat, and rushed out the door.

"Harry, maybe you should go down to your room and try to rest." Harry sat for a few more minutes and then made the decision to take Ron up on the offer. He went down the stairs, closed the door to his room and fell to his knees beside the bed. "Lord, I thank you for Pastor Nick and for those who are going to pray 'bout this. I thank you for Ron and Betty who are letting me stay here. I thank you for your love for me, I'm not good enough but you still love me. Thank you, Thank you!" He got ready for bed and crawled under the covers.

    ***

Tap – tap -tap. "Harry! Harry! Are you awake? Breakfast is ready! Betty is waiting!"

Harry rubbed his eyes and saw that it was daylight. He had slept right through the night! He felt refreshed and ready for the day. At the breakfast table, Ron prayed and read some verses *from Eph. 1:4- 6 "Even before he made the world, God loved us and chose us in Christ to be holy and without fault in his eyes. God decided in advance to adopt us into his own family by bringing us to himself through Jesus Christ. This is what he wanted to do, and it gave him great pleasure. So we praise God for the glorious grace he has poured out on us who belong to his dear Son. He is so rich in kindness and grace that he purchased our freedom with the blood of his Son and forgave our sins."*

"Harry, do you hear what the Lord is saying? You are in God's family, not because of who you are or what you've done, it's because God wanted to have you in His family. We've made the choice to have you in our family. You can stay here just as long as you need to. Together with our church family we'll help you find another job. We believe in you!"

Harry stared at Ron and then at Betty who was nodding in agreement. "You mean I can stay here for free? Why would you do that?"

Betty added, "Because Jesus has spoken to us by His Holy Spirit during the night. We want to obey the Lord and He's told us to let you stay here. We'll expect you to help out around here, just like if you were an uncle. That means helping with yard work or chores inside the house. Does that make sense to you?"

Harry contemplated this idea. He hadn't been in a real family since he was a little boy. He wasn't sure he knew how to be part of a real family.

"Betty, I thank you for your offer, but I don' know how to be part of a family. Being homeless an' drinkin' all the time don't exactly help a guy know how to live in a family. You need to teach me." He wiped tears that were about to trickle down his cheeks, then continued. "You know, a way back when I was runnin' from everything and everybody, I stayed one night with a young couple that were pastors in another town. They wanted me to stay with them, but I was scared and got out of there the next day. God was trying to get my attention then, but I wasn't ready to listen. I had more to learn before I finally gave in and gave my life to the Lord. I think I'd like to be your uncle for a while. But I need lots of help!"

"We also want you to become part of our church family. There are people who really care about you, even if you don't know them. We'll introduce you to some of them along the way. Ron has some connections at his job at the sawmill. When he goes to work later, he'll check out the bulletin board to see if there are any job postings." Betty began clearing the dishes from the table.

Harry jumped up and took some things to the counter and sink. "Do you want me to wash these dishes? That's something I can do."

Ron grinned and gave Betty a kiss before he left. Harry didn't know why, but a thought of Leda flitted through his mind. He quickly pushed that idea down and focused on the task in front of him.

Steve

OVER THE NEXT weeks Harry began to learn how to be part of a real family. He noticed Ron and Betty weren't perfect, they had their little spats, but tried to make up and forgive each other when things got rough. At the Sunday services, he met a few people who didn't look at him sideways, but rather, seemed to care about him as a person. He appreciated that. Then they met with about ten people during the week. He began to look forward to those gatherings. There were times when the separate small groups met for a large potluck in someone's home. Those times were extra special. He found himself feeling comfortable around this larger 'family'.

In the meantime, Ron and some others from the church continued searching for a job for Harry. They weren't having much luck. The minute they revealed they were looking on behalf of Harry, they got the 'cold shoulder'. Harry went out looking for a job every day too. *Lord, you know I need a job! I can't stay at Ron and Betty's for free forever! I'm tryin' to trust you, but it's downright tough!*

One day, he stopped by the café for a coffee in hopes of seeing Leda. It turned out to be his lucky day; she was there! The group of nasty men were there too. Harry wasn't sure how he was going to handle that, but he sat down at a table anyway. Leda came over with the coffee pot and offered him a cup.

"Thanks"

"Haven't seen you around for a while, how's it going?" she asked.

Oh, fine." He couldn't think of anything more to say.

She began to walk back to the kitchen and the group of men made a sarcastic remark about her trying to befriend an Indian. She ignored them and disappeared. Harry drank his coffee slowly and looked out the window. He saw a scruffy guy sitting across the street, near an open doorway. He looked closer and recognized Ally. He had forgotten all about him. Leda came back with the coffee pot, Harry gave her a Toonie and left. He heard the men making rude comments about him, but he didn't care.

"Hi Ally! Haven' seen you 'round for a while. How are you doin'?"

Ally looked up at Harry and shrugged. "What's it to you? I'm survivin".

"Where are you stayin' at night? Do you have a place?" No response. Harry asked again.

"Yeah, I sleep in an old van when it gits too cold. I'm fine."

Harry remembered the many times he'd been in that exact same situation and how blessed he was to have a place to stay now. Yet, he felt helpless to offer Ally anything better than an old van.

Harry leaned against the wall. "A few years ago, I was on the streets all the time. Didn' have no family, no friends, 'cept other drunks. We each had to make do the best we could. That was before I met some guys in a shelter. They let me sleep there and let me help 'round the place during the day. All the while they kept talking about Jesus, and how Jesus was the answer to my loneliness and cravings. I didn't believe 'em at first, but I saw they were different. Some of them had been on the streets too but weren't drinkin' any-more or cussin' or angry like I was. The longer I stayed, the more I was convinced that what they were talkin' about was real."

"Don' give me that religion stuff! I told you before, I didn' want to hear it! Git outta my way, I'm fine!" Ally stood up, shook his hat, placed it over his long straggly hair, and staggered down the street.

Harry watched him go and said a prayer that someday Ally would be ready to listen to who Jesus was – that He wasn't just a 'religion'.

The next Sunday Harry went with Ron and Betty to church. After the service they were having a potluck din-ner. Betty had brought a couple of dishes to share. Everyone lined up and had their plates filled to overflowing. Harry was trying to watch his diet because Betty had been read-ing the books the nurses had given them at the hospital. She showed him how a diet for Diabetes is just a healthy diet, not a big monster that you avoid. He had to admit he was feeling better. The diet plus walking every day and the medication were working. He found a spot to sit with some other fellows and listened to their conversation.

"What about you Harry, what have you been up to?" one of them inquired.

"Oh, I been lookin' for a job, but it's tough in this town."

Ron spoke up, "Yeah, we've been looking everywhere, but keep getting turned down. Seems like people think Indigenous people are lazy no-good bums. Do any of you guys know where Harry could get a job?" Some looked sympathetic but didn't have any suggestions.

Harry noticed a fellow sitting near the end of the ta-ble not saying much. He looked to be in his forties, short dark hair, and medium build. He didn't interact with those around him, just ate his food and scanned the room every so often.

When they were done eating, some said they had to get home to watch the football game and left. The man at the end of the table continued to sit quietly. Harry didn't have anywhere to go because Betty was busy in the kitchen helping to clean up. He noticed some of the young guys starting to put the tables and chairs away, so got up to help. Just then, the quiet man motioned for Harry to come over. Harry acknowledged his invitation and put a chair on the trolley, then sat down across from the man.

"Hi, my name's Harry."

The man seemed to scrutinize him up one side and down the other. Harry was beginning to feel a bit nervous; the man hadn't said a word. Harry fumbled with a napkin that was left on the table and shifted his feet.

"So, I hear you're looking for work." The man said in a raspy voice. "What kind of work do you do?"

Harry cleared his dry throat and squirmed. "I've worked on a couple farms doing chores and other jobs. One place didn't need me no more an' the other place - the owner got sick and ended up in the hospital."

Harry wasn't sure if he should mention the lumber-yard. This town was not small, but gossip travelled around. The man kept staring at him as though he was in deep thought. Harry decided to tell him the rest. "I was working at the lumberyard, but the owner thought I was nothing but trouble and told me to get lost." He felt better as soon as he said it. He knew he had to tell the truth about his past.

More silence. The clean-up crew was closing in on their table. It was becoming evident they needed to get out of the way.

The man said, "Come with me, maybe I've got a job for you."

"Where you goin'?" He wasn't sure he could trust this guy, but then again, what did he have to lose?

"Just wait, I've got to tell Betty and Ron I'm goin' with you." Betty nodded and kept on cleaning up. Ron was running the vacuum cleaner, turned it off and listened to Harry. The look on his face was skeptical but he just said, "Okay, Harry, see you later."

They walked to the door, across the empty parking lot. to the man's car. Harry was getting more nervous by the minute. *Why am I trustin' this guy? Who is he? What's he up to? Is it safe to go with him? Just because he was in church don' mean he's okay.* They stood by the car and Harry kept wondering what was going to happen next. He felt like the man was very unhappy or angry about something. *Lord, can I trust him?* He felt a spirit of peace flow over him and relaxed a bit.

"So, you're looking for a job?" The man asked again. "I heard about the trouble over at the lumberyard, not sure what to think about that."

Harry shrugged; he didn't have a comment.

"My name's Steve. Let's go for a drive."

Harry raised his eyebrows and glanced sideways at the guy. But he walked around to the passenger side and got in. "Nice car. Have you had it long?"

Steve put the car into gear and turned out of the parking lot, "It's about ten years old but it still drives good."

Harry observed that they were driving in an unfamiliar part of town. Soon they were in an industrial area. Steve drove by a few businesses and turned into the parking lot of a nondescript group of buildings. There was a small sign on the door, but nothing else to identify what type of business it was.

"Here we are. This is my shop." They got out of the car and Steve went to the door, inserted a key, and opened it. When the lights were turned on Harry was amazed to see a large photocopier machine, stacks of something (not sure what they were), and a couple of computers.

"Welcome to 'Time For Change Newspaper.'" Harry stood there speechless. "Come." Steve walked ahead. They came to the back of the large room and Steve went into a small room serving as an office.

"Here, sit down."

Harry sat on the chair near the door. Steve plunked himself behind the desk and shuffled some papers out of the way. He looked out the window and then back at Harry. Harry could feel the wheels turning in Steve's head. He waited.

"I was thinking about hiring another person to help here in the shop. To do things like cleaning up, helping lift the cases of paper, and maybe getting the papers ready for delivery, besides other odd jobs. Do you think you could do that?"

Harry gulped. "You mean you'd trust me? I'm willin' to do anythin',"

"Yes, I'd trust you. You see, I haven't always had it good either. I might not look like it, but I'm 'half' and I know how hard it can be to get accepted in a community."

Harry stared at Steve. *For sure, Steve didn' look anythin' but white. Guess a guy can't go by looks.* Harry sat back in the chair and relaxed. Steve pulled some papers out of a drawer and shoved them across the desk.

"Look at these. In fact, take them home and read them over. It's a job application and also an outline of what my business is about and what I'm trying to do in this town." They talked for a few minutes and then Steve asked where Harry lived. Harry explained about Ron and Betty.

"I can take you back to the church and then you can show me where Ron and Betty's place is from there." He stood up. Harry stood up, clutching the papers in his hand.

Back at the house, Harry went to his room after greeting Ron and Betty. He didn't have much to say, he was deep in thought.

He sat on the easy chair in the corner and unfolded the papers. He saw that the name of Steve's company was "Time For Change". *Hm...that's interestin'.* He began reading the mission and purpose of Steve's business. As he read, he got more interested. Steve was actually wanting to begin a new way of thinking in Cortina. The last two pages were an application form for employment. Harry looked them over and decided he needed to talk to Ron and Betty about this.

"Come sit down, Harry." Ron saw that he was holding some papers in his hands.

"Guess you know I went with that guy after the potluck."

"Yes, we wondered what that was all about. That fellow hasn't been coming to our church for very long, don't know much about him. What's his name?"

"His name is Steve. We drove way out into the business area to a small shop hidden in a multiplex building. I couldn't read the name above the door because it was kinda dusty and dirty. I was almost scared because I didn' know this guy. Inside he has a huge photocopier machine, computers, and stacks of paper. He's a man of few words, but he kinda offered me a job and gave me these papers to look over." He handed them to Ron.

Ron scanned them briefly and gave them to Betty. "This is very interesting. I wonder what Pastor Nick knows about Steve? Would you like to talk to him about it?"

"Yeah, I guess so, won' hurt, will it?"

Ron went into the office and called the pastor. "He and his wife will come over for coffee this evening. We can discuss it with him then."

When Pastor Nick and Rhonda had arrived and talked for a while, Harry gave them the papers from Steve. They also looked them over and were quiet for a few minutes.

"I'm not sure what to say, Harry. I've only talked to Steve a couple of times. I didn't know he had a business. He's very quiet, seems to sit and listen most of the time, but I'm sure he's doing a lot of thinking. What do you think about his offer?"

"You know I bin lookin' for a job for a while now, this feels like it's an answer to prayer, but I'm not sure. Steve told me he understands where I've been, 'cause he's been there himself, says he's 'half', but he don' look it."

"I didn't know that, but it doesn't make any difference to me at all. I see him as a person who needs a friend."

Ron spoke up, "I tried to talk with him at church but it's hard when there's so many people milling around. He only responded to my questions and didn't offer any other information about himself."

The group sat deep in thought. "How about we pray about this right now? The Lord knows the desires of our hearts and He knows about your situation Harry."

Each one prayed for direction, protection, and wisdom for Harry as to whether this was the answer to their prayers.

When Harry opened his eyes, he looked at each one and said a simple, "Thank you".

After coffee and a snack, Nick and Rhonda left. Betty was finished putting things away and sat down across from Harry. "I was thinking. How about I take you over to Steve's shop tomorrow and talk to him and sort of check out the place. Women have a 'sixth sense' about things, you know!" She giggled and Ron nodded.

"Good idea! See you in the mornin'." Harry left and went to his room.

A New Job!

ALL NIGHT HE slept off and on. Every time he woke up, he prayed about Steve and the job offer. By morning he felt at peace and looked forward to what the day would hold.

Harry tried to show Betty where Steve's shop was, but he wasn't very good at directions. Then he remembered the papers and searched for the address, while they were stopped at a service station.

"Here's the address! Sorry! I should have told you that in the first place."

"I could have asked too! Let's see." Betty looked at the address and put it into her smart phone. "Oh, we're way off track! We're going the wrong way. I'll turn around and get going to that address."

It took about ten minutes to get onto the right street, but they finally found it. Betty agreed the name above the door wasn't very legible. They got out and knocked on the door. At first there was no answer, but after knocking again, more loudly, Steve cautiously opened the door.

"Oh! It's you! Wasn't expecting anyone."

"This is my landlady, Betty." Harry said. "I was wantin' to talk to you a bit more about this job and Betty offered to bring me over. Sorry we didn't call ahead."

Steve opened the door wider and motioned for them to come in. Betty took a quick survey of the large space.

"Looks like you have quite the setup here, Steve. How long have you been doing this?"

Steve was walking to his office, and they followed. He managed to find another chair from somewhere.

"I've been in this space about a year now. I came from Parktown. I had a business over there for about five years but felt like it was time to move on. I came looking for a church that has a heart for the street people and is actually doing something to help them. I haven't been at your church very many times, but I like what I'm hearing. Then at the potluck I heard this guy here saying he needed a job. I could use some help."

"I see. How often do you print your paper and where do you sell it? I haven't noticed it around town, at least not in the places I've been." Betty kept looking at the cluttered desk and then at a picture in a frame on the wall.

Steve didn't answer right away, so she asked, "Who's that in the picture? They look pretty young?"

"Yes, that's my two kids when they were little. They're all grown up now, haven't seen them for a long time, not even sure where they are." He busied himself with some papers.

Harry ventured a comment. "Yeah I know how that is. I've got a girl somewhere too, but lost track of her a long time ago. Guess that's what the Bible means when it says, 'You'll reap what you sow'.

Betty changed the subject. "How many hours can you offer Harry? And how will he get to work? I work too, so I can't bring him every day."

Again, Steve was quiet for a long time. Harry was getting impatient. *Just spit it out! Betty don' have all day!*

He looked at Harry. "I can offer you four hours a day for now, until I see what kind of work you do and if I can depend on you. The last guy I had quit after a day or so. Don't know why."

Betty interrupted, "Do you have any references from the last town you were in? It would be helpful in making a decision." Harry nodded in agreement, relief on his face.

"Yeah, you can contact this man, he knows me pretty well." He dug a tattered business card out of a desk drawer and gave it to Betty. Harry looked at it too and his eyes almost popped out of his head. He read the name on the card once and then again. Could it be?

"We need to get going." Betty stood up and tucked the card in her purse. "We'll be in touch."

Harry didn't have a chance to say anything about the business card. On the way home he asked to see it again, just to be sure he wasn't dreaming. It definitely read, "Leo Jackson" and had a scripture verse under his name. There was a phone number under that, but the card was so worn, it was hard to see the whole number.

"Guess what, Betty? I recognized the name on this card! Can you believe it?"

She slowed the car down as they neared the house. "Really? How can that be? I think the address on the back was a town about 150 kilometers from here."

"That's right. I lived in that town for over a year. That guy Leo was the one who helped me get straightened out. He had been praying for me for a long time when I landed at the shelter. God sure had His hand on my life and now it's like a miracle that Steve knows Leo too."

Betty stopped the car in front of the house.

"Can I use your house phone to call Leo? I'll try not to make it too long."

"Go ahead, we've got a flat rate for long distance."

Harry got out. "See you later. God bless!" and she was off.

Harry looked at the phone number and decided it was clear enough to read. His hand shook as he dialed the number. Ring...ring... ring... Click. *Maybe it wasn't the right number. He expected a message or something.* He looked at the card once more. *Maybe that's a seven, not a one, I'll try that.*

Ring...ring...ring...ring...ring...ring... Harry was holding his breath. Ring...ring...ring... "Hello this is Leo..." Harry started talking but then realized he was talking to a machine, so after the beep he left a message and his number.

Harry noticed the kitchen hadn't been cleaned up when they left in such a hurry. He swept the floor, washed the dishes, and tidied up the counter, then went to his room and pulled out his Bible. The part he had been reading the day before seemed to fit right into his situation.

He opened it back up to Psalm chapter 62, verses five to eight and thoughtfully read

"But I stand silently before the Lord, waiting for him to rescue me. For salvation comes from Him alone. Yes, He alone is my Rock, my rescuer, defense, and fortress—why then should I be tense with fear when troubles come?

My protection and success come from God alone. He is my refuge, a Rock where no enemy can reach me. O my people, trust Him all the time. Pour out your longings before Him, for He can help!"

"Yes, Lord! You know all 'bout my situation and you know 'bout Steve and Leo and the people I've come to know here. I put my trust in you today, for you to show me the right path. Thank you, Jesus!"

The phone rang while they were eating supper. Harry's heart leaped – maybe it was Leo! Ron went to answer it but talked a while and then came back to the table.

"Some marketing guy wanting to know if I could donate to a charity – as if!"

"How was your day, Harry? Did you get in touch with the guy whose name was on the card?"

"No, I left a message though, I hope he calls back." Harry was feeling a bit discouraged. "So, Betty, what did you think of Steve?"

She chose her words carefully. "I think he's probably a pretty good guy even though his place was in quite a mess. I could see he needed some help. Maybe after you talk to this Leo fellow, you'll be able to make a decision."

Harry nodded.

"By the way, Harry, did you read some of those booklets from the Diabetes Clinic?"

Harry hung his head. "Uh...no...didn't have time." Then he thought *that's not true! I had all day!* "Um, I mean...I mean...no, I didn't."

"Do you need help to understand what it's all about? I can try and help you if you want."

"Okay, that would be good, thanks. I'll go and get them later."

He helped clear the table and then went to his room. He dug through the papers in a bag and found the package from the clinic. *Guess I better try to sort through this stuff. I still think they're wrong, I don' have Diabetes, I feel fine!*

Upstairs, Betty opened a booklet, scanned a few pages and asked Harry if he knew what it was saying.

"Not so much." In the back of his mind, he wasn't ready to accept the diagnosis.

Betty went back to the beginning of the booklet and began reading a few paragraphs at a time, then she would stop and ask if he understood it. Harry would nod but didn't offer any comments. Betty was getting a bit frustrated.

"Harry! I'm trying to help you! Do you want help or not?"

"I don't believe I've got this sickness! I don't want to learn about it!" He was pushing his chair back from the table. Ron had overheard the conversation and came into the kitchen.

"Harry, we know this is hard. Betty has been reading up on this and she can see where you can have high sugars for a long time and not even know it. At the same time, the sugars can make you easily upset, angry, and very tired. Maybe you could try a little harder?"

Harry said. "Speaking of tired. I'm tired. I'm going to bed." He stuffed the booklet and papers in the bag and hurried down the stairs.

Before crawling under the covers, he knelt beside the bed and poured out his heart to the Lord. "Lord, I don' know about this sickness, and I don't want to know about it! I don't need this in my life. I'm out of a job and everything is going wrong."

Lying on his pillow the Bible verses he had read in the morning came back to him *"My protection and help comes from God alone."* He was trying to trust, but it was so hard!

A Surprise Encounter

NEXT MORNING RON and Betty went to work before Harry was up. He made himself some breakfast and read the note they had left. "No one called last night." He was more discouraged and more tired than ever. He looked out the window and saw that it was raining. *Just like my heart - it's raining in there too.* The dark and dreary day wasn't helping his mood. Somehow, he had to get himself in a better frame of mind. He needed to get out of the house. Do something! He put on a windbreaker jacket and cap and went out the door, locking it behind him. He walked in the direction of the café. In the back of his mind, he thought about Leda. *Maybe he could talk to her or at least see her.*

When he entered the café, he noticed the usual group of men were absent. He looked at his watch and knew that they came much earlier in the morning. He breathed a sigh of relief - he didn't need their rude comments. He sat down and waited and sure enough, Leda came out of the kitchen.

"Hi. Good to see you." she said. "How about a coffee?"

Harry was dazzled by her blue eyes. "Uh...yes please!"

She poured the coffee and stood there for a minute, like she was waiting for him to say something.

Harry gulped and responded, "Yeah, guess you heard about the big thing at the lumberyard. I don't have a job no more."

Leda nodded. "I heard about it. I don't believe what they're saying about you."

"Really? How come?"

"You just seem like a decent kind of guy. I think Percy got all twisted up by his so called 'friends'. I saw that you went to work every day faithfully."

"You did?" Harry was surprised. "Why would you notice that?"

"Oh, I don't know, just did."

Harry got a little less nervous. "I saw you at church the other Sunday, do you go there much?"

"I try to, but sometimes I have to work on Sundays. Just depends on my schedule."

"Oh, that makes sense." There was an awkward pause.

"I better get back to the kitchen. Things to do before the lunch crowd comes in."

Harry finished his coffee, He was feeling better already! Leda seemed to lift his spirits just by taking time to talk for a minute. He wandered down the street but couldn't find anyone to visit or anything to do, so he went back home.

All during the day, he wrestled with himself, flipping between his feelings for Leda, that he couldn't understand and telling himself she wouldn't care for him. Then he also fought with the diagnosis of Diabetes. Finally, he opened the booklet Betty had been reading and read the first pages. *Lord, you know about this here diagnosis. If it's true, help me understand this stuff.* He had to read the first part over more than once but gradually he began to get what it was saying. He had to admit that the symptoms they were describing had been in his body too. He thought back to the previous weeks and months. The surges of anger that were actually uncalled for, the tiredness, and the weight he had put on.

He read some more. The booklet was explaining how a high
sugar level could cause these feelings. He got stuck on one
part. *I'll let Betty explain that to me, I guess.*

Later, Betty sat down with Harry again. This time he
was more agreeable and listened as she went over the booklet.

"You see, Harry, if the sugar levels go down by watching
your diet, exercising, and taking the pills the doctor gave
you, you will find that you start feeling different. It takes
a long time to get high sugars so it can take a long time to
get them down, but it can happen."

Harry sat back and thought about it. "Guess you're
right. I been kinda edgy for a long time, didn't know why.
Thought I was just getting old and cranky!" he laughed.

Betty showed him how she was trying to make meals
that were healthy for him but told him it was up to him
about the other stuff, like walking and taking his pills.

"Yeah, I left those pills in the bottle, thought I could get
along without them. But I did go for a walk today!"

"That's great, Harry. Glad to hear that."

"Did you get a call from Leo yet? I thought he would
have called back by now."

"Oh! I forgot! I was busy making supper and then going over this booklet. Sorry! Yes, there was a message on
the phone. He said he'd call later tonight. Sorry!"

Harry was relieved to hear this. He glanced at the clock
and saw that it was getting near 10:00 pm, Leo wouldn't
be calling this late. "Better let you guys get to bed. Thanks
for your help. G'night."

Harry was in the middle of getting ready for bed when
Ron knocked on his door. "Harry! Leo is on the phone!"

Harry ran to the door and Ron handed him the portable phone. "Hello? Hello? Is that you Leo?" Harry listened
intently. "Really? Is that right? Oh no!"

"Thanks for calling. It's getting' late, I'd better let these people get to bed. God bless you!"

He handed the phone to Ron and smiled. "Leo has been away for a while. He didn't get the message till today. He's gonna call again tomorrow. Thanks." It had been good to talk to Leo. Leo was a positive guy, who always looked at things on the bright side – just what Harry needed!

Harry stayed around the house all the next day but didn't hear the phone ring. By afternoon, he knew he better get outside and walk. The rain had stopped, and the air was fresh with the aroma of trees and flowers. This time he intentionally noticed the neat houses and yards around Ron and Betty's place. People obviously took a lot of time to keep their yards looking nice.

A few steps down the next block he saw an elderly man on his knees working in his flower garden.

"G'day sir! How are you?" Harry called from the side-walk.

 The old man looked up and then carefully stood up. He sized Harry up and down and responded. "Good day to you! I'm fine! I love digging in my garden. It's good therapy for the soul."

Harry didn't know how digging in the dirt could be therapy, but he nodded. "Do you ever need any help with the diggin'?" Harry wasn't sure where that idea came from, but he liked it. "I could use some therapy myself!"

The man walked over to Harry, took off his glove and extended his hand. "My name's John, but most of the time I'm called 'Ole Johnny'. Glad to meet you."

Harry shook his hand, "My name's Harry. I live down the street there." He pointed to a house at the far end of the block.

"I've seen you walk by now and then but didn't know you lived around here. As a matter of fact, yes, I could use some help. This old body doesn't want to work like it used to, gets pretty stiff and sore, even though I like to work out here."

"I ain't never done any gardenin', but I'm willin' to learn if you show me what to do."

Ole Johnny thought for a minute. "I just might consider that. How about you come over tomorrow morning around 8:00 before the sun gets too hot. I'll think about what I need done overnight."

"That sounds great, thank you! I'll be here!"

Harry continued down the block. When he came to the end, he turned to his right onto an unfamiliar street. For some reason, he hadn't ever noticed these houses and other buildings before. He walked for another fifteen minutes, not taking notice of exactly where he was. There was an apartment building with three floors alongside houses that were badly in need of repair. It was in stark contrast to where Ron and Betty lived. He was almost past the apartment building when he heard his name. *Who would know his name over here?* He stopped in his tracks and cautiously turned around. He was startled to see Leda by the door of the apartment.

"Harry! What are you doing in this part of town?"

Harry retraced his steps, looked at Leda with astonishment. "What are YOU doing in this part of town?"

"I live here. I was just going to the grocery store. Where are you going?"

"Don't know, just walking. Needed to get some fresh air and exercise."

"How about you come with me to the store?"

Harry hesitated and then said, "Okay, got nothing else to do right now. Thanks."

At the store, Harry let Leda go in, he didn't want to make her uncomfortable. To put in time, he went to a store next door and looked around. After a half hour, he came out and sat on a bench near the entrance of the grocery store.

"All done, thanks for waiting." Leda was carrying a couple of obviously heavy tote bags. Harry jumped up and offered to carry them.

"Oh, I'm fine, but here, you can carry one. There's a coffee shop across the street, how about we go and have a coffee?"

"Uh... Uh..." Harry tried to come up with an excuse, but he didn't really want to make an excuse. "Sure, that'd be good."

When they were seated in the coffee shop, Harry felt uneasy. He wasn't sure how to talk to this beautiful lady, her blue eyes seemed to look right through him. Leda chattered about the weather and a bit about her job, trying to get Harry to relax.

"Yeah, I know about working in places that aren't the best. It gets purty hard sometimes."

"Tell me about where you've been."

"Ah, you wouldn't want to know about where I bin. Too mixed up and messy."

She shared some of her life. Told him about growing up near a reserve in another province and that she had an Indigenous girlfriend all through school. Her name was Patricia, but they both quit after grade ten and went their separate ways.

"I've lost track of her over the years. I often wonder what happened to her."

"Yeah, I know what you mean. I only went to grade eight, couldn't take it no more. The school was on reserve and most of the guys my age figured school was a waste of time, so we went out looking for trouble – and we found it!" He stopped abruptly, grabbed his cup and took a gulp. *Better not tell her too much. She don' need to know about my ugly past.*

"Don't worry, I know all about looking for trouble! I've been there too!"

"You have?? Really?"

All of a sudden, Leda looked at her watch, "Oh my, time is racing on. I need to get home."

Harry offered to carry one tote bag and they were off. They talked non-stop all the way and Harry was feeling more and more comfortable being around her. At the entrance to the apartment, Harry handed the bag to Leda. "Thanks for the visit, see you 'round."

Leda glanced up at him and smiled and nodded. "We need to do this again! Thanks for carrying my groceries." The door clicked behind her and she was gone.

Harry stood there overwhelmed with the turn of events. What were the chances of meeting up with Leda? *Thank you, Lord. I don' know what else to say. Just thank you.* He took note of the street numbers and the apartment number as he made his way back home. He wasn't going to forget that address!

After supper he took the booklet about Diabetes up to Betty and asked her to explain some of the things he didn't understand. This time he was ready to listen and learn, but his mind kept wandering off, seeing Leda's smiling cyes.

"Harry! Are you with me?" Betty was getting annoyed. "You said you wanted to learn this stuff."

"Ah... sorry. I'm having trouble thinking straight, maybe we better call it a day, I'm kinda tired. Oh, by the way. I was talkin' to Ole Johnny down the street this morning. He said he could use some help in his garden, so I'm goin' over tomorrow morning to learn about gardenin'. Do you know him?"

Betty looked up in surprise. "Know him? Yes, I know him!" The statement indicated that she wasn't too fond of Ole Johnny. "He's lived in that house forever! Keeps to himself, won't associate with the neighbours. I'm surprised he even talked to you."

Harry didn't respond, except to wish her 'good night' and head for the basement. *Sure strange how the Lord works!* He read his Bible and prayed for a few minutes, then went to bed.

Learning a New Skill

THE NEXT MORNING, he got up in time to have breakfast with Ron and Betty. Then he went to learn about gardening. He arrived at 8:00 as agreed and found Ole Johnny already at it.

"G-mornin' I see you're busy already.

"Yep, got to get out before it's too hot." He stood up and groaned as he straightened his back. "Didn't think you'd be back!"

"I got nothin' else to do. Besides, I'd like to learn about gardenin'."

"Come with me, I'll show you what needs to be done in the back. This flower bed ain't nothing." He led the way to the back of the house. Harry was shocked to see a huge garden. The whole backyard was covered! "There's lots to do back here, the weeds keep growing right along with all the veggies. Do you know which ones are the weeds?"

Harry shrugged, "Not sure. You better tell me, so I don't pull the wrong thing up."

Ole Johnny walked between the rows and indicated what needed to be taken out. Harry was soon hard at it, down on his hands and knees, putting a pile of weeds at the end of the row every so often. By noon he was getting very thirsty and was already feeling his muscles getting tight. "I need to go home and get something to eat and drink. I'll be back in an hour, if that's okay?"

Ole Johnny was surveying the piles of weeds and nodded. He seemed pleased with Harry's work but didn't say much. "Be back by 1:30."

Harry worked all afternoon. He couldn't believe there was so much work in the place. About the time he thought he was done Ole Johnny would find another spot that he wanted cleaned out. By 5:00 Harry was completely exhausted, he hadn't done so much manual labour in a long time.

"You've done a good job! Thanks. You did much better than I thought you would. Here, thanks for your help." Ole Johnny pulled a roll of bills out of his pocket and handed him four 20s.

"Thank you, thank you! I've been out of job, been lookin' for somethin' to do. Thank you. God bless you!"

A slight smile crossed Ole Johnny's face, then he turned away. "See you around."

Harry took that to mean he wouldn't be needed for a while. After all, he had done a huge amount of work in that one day. He walked home and greeted Betty as he came in the door. Dinner smelled wonderful. He was starving.

"That ole boy sure knows how to make a guy work! Nearly killed me today! I'm so tired, don' know if I can even eat."

"Harry! Sit down, I'll get you some juice and a few crackers, just to get you through till we eat. You need to eat!" She brought the items to the table.

Harry gulped the juice down and then a glass of water. He hadn't taken anything along to eat or drink and he was feeling the effects of it.

"When you take those pills for your Diabetes, you have to eat and drink, especially when you're working hard out in the hot sun. You can get very sick. You don't want to end up in the hospital again, do you?"

Harry shuddered at the thought. He certainly did not want to go there again! "I better go down and get cleaned up."

At the table, they shared about their day.

"Oh, by the way, Steve left a message, he was wondering if you were still interested in the job." Ron handed Harry a piece of paper with a number on it.

"Really? He wants me?" Harry was surprised. "I'll call him in the mornin'. Ole Johnny gave me 80 bucks for helpin' him out today. Here, you can have forty for groceries or whatever. The Lord has provided for me, so you guys are providin' for me, and I appreciate it! But I better keep some for bus fare."

It looked like Betty was about to hand it back but changed her mind. "Ah, Harry, that's sweet of you! Thank you!"

Harry nodded and stood up carefully, he was soooooo sore! "I need to go to bed – not used to this hard labour!"

The next morning Harry could barely get out of bed, his muscles were rebelling! He phoned Steve and agreed to come in later that day. He had to sort out the dilemma of how to get to Steve's shop. He knew there were buses, but he wasn't sure which one to take. The thought came to him *Leda would know! She said she takes the bus to work!* He gathered his things together, including a bag with a sandwich and water that Betty had left for him, and went out the door. At the café he saw the 'club' guys sitting there as usual. He sat down and waited. Soon a different lady came out and offered him coffee. He decided Leda wasn't there. "Sorry, I changed my mind, I have to leave." He heard snide remarks as he went out the door. *Maybe I should go back to the house and phone Steve and ask him which bus to take.*

"Good mornin' Steve! Harry here. I forgot to ask you about how to get to your place on the bus. Which bus do I take?" Harry listened closely and tried to write down the number on the paper. "Thanks, I'll try and be there as soon as I can."

He walked down a different street that had a bus stop; dug change out of his pocket and waited. After a long while, the bus came along. He showed the address of Steve's business to the driver and asked how to get there. He put his money in the box, got a transfer, and sat near the front so he could hear when the driver told him where to get off. He caught the next bus and soon discovered that he was about a five-minute walk to the shop.

He pushed the door open and saw Steve moving some heavy boxes across the floor. Steve turned and saw Harry. "Oh, you made it! I sure can use some help!"

Harry went to the back office, put his coat and lunch down and hurried to help. He couldn't move as fast as usual, because he was so stiff from all the gardening he'd done the day before. As they worked together, there wasn't much time for talking, except when Steve told him what needed to be done next. When they stopped for a break, Steve plopped down on a chair, mopped his brow, and heaved a big groan. "How're you doing? Do you think you can handle this job?"

Harry wasn't sure right then. He was hurting so bad he could hardly think. He explained to Steve about his job the day before and that he was really sore.

"Okay, let's take a break. Did you fill out the papers?"

"Oh yeah, forgot to give them to you. Here. Guess what, I talked to Leo! I didn't know you knew Leo! The Lord sure knows how to work things out, 'specially when a guy don't have all the answers."

Steve nodded and then shared how he had known Leo many years ago. Homeless and starving he had gone to the

shelter to get something to eat. As he got into the habit of
going there every day, the workers began to share about
Jesus. He kept going, but somehow couldn't accept all they
were telling him. Harry would agree every once in a while,
indicating he knew all about it.

"I think we'd better get back to work! I need to get this
week's paper printed." After tidying up from lunch, they
went out to the photocopy machine. Steve showed Harry a
few things to get him started. The afternoon flew by and
Steve announced it was quitting time.

At home, Harry took a few minutes to clean up and
then sat down in the living room with Ron and Betty.

"How did it go today?" Ron questioned. He noticed that
Harry looked tired. "Do you think you can handle working
with Steve?"

"Yeah, we got along real good. It's just great to hear his
story, it's much like mine. I'm so thankful for how the Lord
has worked things out." He gave a big sigh and sat back
on the couch. He tried to stay awake while Ron and Betty
talked, but, in spite of himself, he dozed off.

"Harry! I think you better go to bed!" Betty was shaking his shoulder.

Harry jumped. "Sorry! Didn't mean to go to sleep.
Sorry!" He struggled to his feet and headed for his room.

A Special Lunch Date

THE NEXT DAY was Friday and Harry was glad. He was tired, stiff, and feeling like he was a hundred years old. He and Steve had done a lot of work over two days, but there always seemed to be more to do. He was glad to ride the bus so he could relax for a while. He was beginning to understand what Steve was trying to do. He had told Harry how he was observing relationships in Cortina. How some people seemed to think they were better than others by making rude comments within earshot of the person – just to make sure it was heard. It seemed to Harry that Steve was trying to get some kind of protest going, or rebellion against the 'establishment'; he wasn't sure. In spite of his uneasy feelings about the topics Steve was covering, Harry felt deep down it was time to take action. When he was at home, he told Betty a bit about it, but didn't get into much detail - didn't think it was the time.

Saturday came and Harry found opportunity to sleep in. It felt so good! His muscles weren't quite so sore. He decided maybe the diet and pills were making him feel better – even if he didn't want to admit it. He helped Ron in the yard later in the day and felt good that he had an idea of what to do after working with Ole Johnny.

Sunday morning, he put on his best jeans with a striped navy and white shirt, brushed his short, straight hair and adjusted his glasses. When they arrived at church, he scanned the lobby but didn't see Leda. They sat waiting for the service to begin, but he kept looking over to where Leda usually sat. No luck. He decided he better pay attention to the singing and sermon and not get side-tracked by thinking about her.

Pastor Nick's sermon was about sharing the gospel with your neighbours. "You are here in this place for a reason. Other people's lives depend on you. You aren't alone, living on an island." His words struck deep. Harry thought about Ole Johnny and questioned if he was supposed to share with him. He was deep in thought at the end of the service, praying for clear direction from the Lord. Someone tapped him on the shoulder, and he turned with a start. There was Leda! *Where did she come from?* He was baffled.

"Oh hi!" Was all he could manage to blurt out. He stood up and smiled. Leda, was wearing a white jacket, navy slacks, and a multi-coloured shirt. Her light brown curls were pulled back with a navy hairband.

"Hi. I didn't see you come in this morning. I was in the nursery helping the girls down there. What are you doing after church?"

"Uh... Uh...not sure."

"How about we go for lunch at Mandy's?" her eyes sparkled.

"Oh! I'll check with Ron and Betty. They gave me a ride over."

Betty smiled when Harry told her about Leda. "She's a wonderful lady! I'm glad for you." Harry wondered what that meant – exactly. However, he didn't have time to think about it, because Leda was standing by the door waiting.

"Let's catch the bus, I know which one to take."

On the bus, Leda kept up a lively chatter about what happened at the café last week. She was bouncy and bright, and Harry didn't need to say much. He listened in wonder, as she talked about her encounter with one of the 'club' (the morning coffee guys).

"You know? His name is Peter. He comes in early every morning looking angry and miserable. I joke around with him and soon he brightens up, but when the other guys show up, his mood changes back to being grouchy. Guess he doesn't want them to see him in a good mood or something."

The bus stopped down the street from the restaurant and they got off. Leda could walk really fast, and Harry had trouble keeping up with her, even though his muscles were recovering.

"How about you? How was your week?" She continued as they waited for their order.

Harry told her about Ole Johnny. "He's another one of those grumpy guys, but he seemed to like my work. I started a new job at a sort of print shop. Took the bus down to this guy named Steve. Do you know him? He comes to church sometimes."

Leda shook her head, "No, afraid not. What kind of stuff does he print?"

"It's kind of confusing. I've read some of it, but I'm not sure where he's goin' with it. He has this idea to change this town, to make it better. He sees the discrimination that's happenin' all the time."

Leda looked down and concentrated on her food. "This is so delicious! I'm glad I ordered it. How about yours?"

Harry was finishing the last bite and nodded. "It's purty good, but don't match Betty's cooking. She's trying to teach me how to eat right."

Leda looked up. "Eat right? What do you mean?"

Harry fumbled for words, not sure he wanted to tell Leda about his diabetes -- maybe she'd get rid of him in a hurry. But he decided he couldn't lie to her. "Yeah, they told me I got diabetes." He held his breath and waited for her reaction.

"Really? I've known a few people with it. Not sure how I would feel about being told I had it."

"Yeah. I was mad. I didn't want nobody telling me what to eat or all the other stuff they throw at a guy. It's not easy."

Leda was quiet again, getting real busy with her coffee cup. "What did you think about Pastor Nick's sermon this morning?"

Harry got confused with the sudden change of subject. He racked his brain to remember.

Leda continued when Harry didn't answer right away. "I think he hit the nail on the head. Our lives DO affect everyone around us. We can set the mood and we CAN make a difference by what we talk about. Like - we can waste a lot of time complaining about the weather or about the politicians in power or about how we need a better job. But you know, the Bible tells us to be thankful in all situations and to be joyful."

"Boy! That's hard! I don't do very well in that." He confessed. "But the Lord was telling me I can talk to Ole Johnny next time I see him, tell him 'bout the love of Jesus."

Leda agreed, "I heard the same message about talking to Peter at the café. He needs the Lord too."

They prepared to leave, and each paid for their own meal. Harry felt a bit ashamed about that but was thankful she had suggested it. Steve hadn't paid him yet and funds weren't plentiful.

On the bus, Leda enquired, "So, where are you from anyway? You haven't told me a lot about yourself."

Harry was uncomfortable at first but soon was at ease with her. It felt like he could tell her anything. "I quit school and ended up getting' into trouble big time. Next thing I knew I was in the 'cooler' for some silly actions I did. Things went downhill from there 'till I ended up on the streets."

Leda was quiet for a long time. "Harry, it doesn't matter where you've been in the past, I only see you where you are now. I see you trying to live for the Lord and to do what's right. Would you like me to add you to my prayer list?"

"You have a prayer list?" His eyes wide in surprise. "Why would you wanna add me to your list? Must be other people that need your prayers more."

"Harry, everyone needs someone to pray for them! Remember, the pastor said we aren't an island out there meant to be all alone. We need each other."

"Okay, thanks." Harry couldn't think of anything else to say.

"Here's where I get off, thanks for a good day. Have a good week!" Leda stood up and was gone before Harry could get his wits about him to even say good-bye.

"How was your date?" Ron teased. "She's pretty cute, isn't she?"

Harry squirmed, looked at him and turned away. He had to agree, but he wasn't going to let Ron know that. He tried to think of something to change the subject.

"Sure is hot out there! Wonder if it's gonna bring some rain again.? That'll make Ole Johnny's garden grow big time. I promised him I'd help him out again, but now I'm workin' for Steve, not sure how that's gonna' work."

"Maybe you could do a little bit each evening instead of doing the whole thing in one day. Wouldn't be so hard then."

Harry thought about that and agreed. He would really like to talk to Ole Johnny and get to know him. Maybe talk to him about the Lord, like the pastor was saying. "I think I'll go down and have a rest if you don't mind. Kind of tired for some reason."

In his room, he laid on the bed, but all he could think about was Leda. He kept seeing her beautiful eyes and the way she smiled. No matter how he tried, he couldn't think of anything else. *Maybe if I read a book, I can forget about her. She wouldn' care for me, I'm not good enough for her. Besides, what would I do with a girlfriend? I've forgotten how to act 'round women.* He tossed and turned, then got up and sat in the chair. His attempt to read, was a no-go. *Maybe I'll go for a walk. That'll clear my head.* The minute he stepped out into the fresh air, he felt better. Striding down the street, he was on top of the world. Life was good! *Thank you Lord, for all your blessings!*

He walked in the direction of downtown, thinking he might run into Ally. Soon he was in the area where Ally usually hung out, but no one was in sight. He kept walking, going into another different part of town. He came to a park that he'd never seen before. There were people having a picnic with their kids and a couple walking their dog. He sat down on a bench and watched the little ones playing tag, giggling and taunting each other to be caught.

A memory of his childhood flashed into his mind. His cousins had been so much fun in those days. He felt sad that they were lost and gone forever.

One of the kids ran by him and shouted, "Hi grandpa!" He laughed. "Hi to you too! What's your name?" But the boy was gone, running after a dog on a leash. *Grandpa! Do I look that old? I suppose to a little one I do. Never thought of it before.* He reminded himself that he *was* 48 years old. About time he settled down with a wife. *What?? Where did that come from? That's crazy!* He stood up and stomped back up the path he had come. He wasn't interested in a wife.

Back at the house, Betty called to him when he got in the door. "Supper is soon ready!"

"Okay, thanks, I'll be right up."

At the table he told them about finding the park and how the little boy called him 'Grandpa'. He laughed, "Maybe I am a grandpa and don' know it!"

"What do you mean by that?" Betty asked.

"Guess I didn't tell you -- I have a girl somewhere. Lost track of her a long time ago. She lived in another province. Who knows where she might be now?"

"Oh, I'm sorry, Harry, that must be really hard. Our girls live in another province, but we hear from them all the time and from our grandsons too. They are just four and six, but they're so cute on the phone. Did I ever show you some pictures of them?" She ran to the living room and brought back an album. "Look, here they are playing at the splash park near where they live."

Harry watched as she turned the pages and pointed out different scenes. He could tell she was very proud of them. "They sure are cute! Do they come here sometimes?"

"No, not often. We have to travel to them because they're so busy with work and all." She was suddenly sad.

"Yeah, guess I know a bit 'bout missing family." They looked at a few more pictures and then Harry decided it was time for bed. "Thanks for supper. It was good! G'night!"

Harry's Very Own Apartment!

ALL THAT WEEK he worked for Steve in the daytime and a couple of times he stopped by Ole Johnny's after supper. Things were going along very well. He was glad for a job and glad for new friends.

At church the next Sunday, he searched for Leda, but didn't see her, then he remembered she helped in the nursery. He hoped he would see her before he left. He listened closely to the pastor as he spoke about only one God and only one way to heaven. Pastor Nick read from John 14, that says, "Jesus is the way, the truth and the life, not just 'a' way, but the only way." He praised the Lord in his heart that Leo and the other guys had led him to *the* way.

"Hi, how are you doing?" Leda was standing beside him. He jumped and turned toward her. Seemed like she always caught him off-guard.

"Sorry, didn't mean to scare you!"

"Oh, that's okay, I was just waitin' for Ron and Betty. How was it with the little ones today?"

"Busy! They have so much energy, wish I had that much get-up and go! How was your week?"

"Yeah, it was busy, but it was a good kind of busy. I managed to work in Ole Johnny's garden a couple of evenings and he seemed to appreciate it. Tryin' to get to know him."

 "How about we go for lunch again? I liked that."

Harry's eyes grew big. "Really? Sure, I'd like that. I'll let my folks know. I'll be right back." He looked across the group in the foyer and spotted Ron.

Ron nodded when Harry told him where he was going and gave him a little nudge, "Better keep that one on the line!" He winked.

During lunch Harry and Leda shared more about where they were from. Leda told him she grew up in a small farming community about five hours away. She had not finished school. Got to grade 10 and quit. "I was bored and my friends that weren't in school were having so much more fun." Her parents had died in an accident when she was seventeen and she had been left to find her own way in life. She told him about being in a bad relationship with a guy that turned into being very scary. The man threatened to beat her if she didn't do *what* he wanted and *when* he wanted, so she got out before it got worse. He also drank a lot, which was not her style at all. "I left that town and started looking for work in different places, ended up here in Cortina. My education and work experience don't make it easy to get a high paying job, so I settled for being a waitress."

"You do a great job as a waitress." Harry exclaimed. "Don't ever put yourself down! But I'm wonderin' when Jesus came into your life."

Leda smiled. "Glad you asked. It was when I was searching for something that was missing in my life that I landed here. I noticed that a certain man would come into the café a couple times a week, often with different guys, not just the same buddies all the time. I overheard their conversations about Jesus and started to ask myself questions about who Jesus was. Then the 'regular guy' introduced himself as Pastor Nick and invited me to Sunday service and gave me his card with the address. After attending a few Sundays, I began to realize the emptiness I felt was a spiritual thing, not a physical one. Three years ago, I made the decision to invite Jesus into my heart. It was the best decision I've ever made in my life!" Her dazzling smile threw Harry into a spin. He felt a true connection with her.

"Oh! Look at the time! I better be getting home! I've got lots of things to do before I go to the café in the morning."

On the bus, Harry felt the heat of her body beside him, and he got all tingly inside.

"Bye Harry, have a good week."

"Bye, see you." After she got off, he was so busy in his thoughts about Leda that he almost missed his stop.

Ron teased him unmercifully about his date and Harry got all flustered and felt like a teenager. *I'm too old to be in love. That's for the young uns. Besides, Leda is too good for me.* All afternoon and evening he went through the same tussle with his thoughts as last week. *What am I gonna do with this woman? Lord, help!!*

The Sunday lunch with Leda went on for a few weeks and they soon exchanged phone numbers. They began to understand each other better and Harry looked forward to seeing her more and more. They talked on the phone whenever they could, and Harry had to admit to himself that he was having deep feelings for her. His job with Steve was getting into a routine too. He got to know what Steve wanted even before he asked for something to be done and Steve said he appreciated his help. When pay day came, Harry was over-joyed to see how much he had earned. He even went down to the bank and set up an account. It felt good! His relationship with Ole Johnny was growing too.

Working in the garden turned out to be very satisfying, just like Ole Johnny said. If Harry was frustrated about something, digging in the dirt helped him to work out that emotion. The exercise and the change in diet was making a difference. His blood sugars were now normal, and he began to realize he hadn't been feeling well for a long time. Betty continued to help him make the right food choices and what to look for in the grocery stores, so he didn't waste a lot of money on junk food.

One day, Harry woke up and suddenly remembered it was the beginning of October. The summer had been good. His wages from Steve and Ole Johnny had been growing in his bank account and he felt he was ready to move out of Ron and Betty's. He looked through the papers and also asked Steve about places for rent. He went to a couple, but the minute they saw he was Indigenous, they said the apartment was not available.

Much to his chagrin, he had to admit he couldn't do it alone and thought about asking Leda if she could help him, but he knew he couldn't let her fight his battles. They were his. *Maybe I'd better ask Pastor Nick about helping me find a place. He knows more people around here than I do.*

Eventually, Pastor Nick went with Harry, and they found an apartment that was suitable. Some of the church people helped him get furniture and basic supplies that he needed to survive on his own. He missed Ron and Betty, but he had to get on with his life. Somehow, getting on with his life kept including Leda. His thoughts and emotions were in a continual ebb and flow. Some days he wanted to ask her to marry him, some days he reprimanded himself and said it was a bad idea.

When the first snow began falling, he stopped by Ole Johnny's place after work. "Guess the yard work is done for this year." They were having a cup of coffee in the kitchen.

Ole Johnny nodded, "Yeah, time to relax a bit. You know, Harry, you've been a great help to me this summer. I couldn't have stayed in this place without your help. My old bones can't take the hard work anymore. I suppose one of these times, I'll have to move somewhere else, but I don't want to. All my memories are in this house and yard. Things were going along good until my missus – her name was Matilda – up and died on me. The emptiness of the house nearly drove me to drink, in fact I did drink for a while."

"I know what you mean. I'm living in an apart-ment now, and I miss being at Ron and Betty's but I know that I have to learn to live alone. I tried the drinkin' thing for a lot of years. It didn' work. I ended up on the streets, lost and homeless. But then I found Jesus! Some guys at a homeless shelter showed me the way to true happiness. It's not about trustin' in people, or government leaders, or in our money, it's about trustin' Jesus for every hour of every day. I've found out that's the only way to get through the tough times and even the good times." Ole Johnny didn't answer, but he was obviously thinking.

"What do you mean, 'You found Jesus'?"

"Well, I was reading in my Bible about how God has planted eternity in the hearts of human beings, and I knew that somethin' was missin' in my life until I gave up goin' my own way and gave my heart and life to Jesus. He filled that empty space in my life. When I really looked for Jesus, I realized He had been there with me all the time. I just didn' know it."

"Yeah, I'm old now. I think I heard about Jesus way back in my early years, but I was too busy making a living, getting married, and looking in all the wrong places for happiness. Matilda made life worth living but something was missing. Work didn't make me happy although I en-joyed working in a hardware store. It was good to meet lots of people and to be able to help them out. But when I had to retire, I was lonesome for the contact with people. Then when Matilda died, I got real bitter and mad at God. That's kind of funny, because I had no time for God through my life, but yet I got mad at Him for how my life was.

Harry prayed a quick prayer. "You know God can handle you bein' mad at Him. He knows you better than you know yourself. But my Bible tells me He loved me so much – and you – that He let His Son be killed. But that's not the end of the story! Jesus died for you and me, He's alive! He rose from the dead!"

Ole Johnny hung his head. After a while, he looked at Harry. "Yeah, I have to admit I heard that story when I was a kid. My Mom tried to tell me about Jesus, but I didn't want to listen. My Dad was the macho kind, always bragging and claiming he didn't need Jesus or anybody to help him. He could do it all himself. Mom took me and my brother away when I was about twelve because she couldn't live with my dad and his attitude. She had taken us to church all the time, but my dad just ranted at her about it. That's why I ran away from Mom and school when I was fourteen, went to my Dad. It took about six months before I found out there was no happiness with him, just boozing, fighting, and working, so I moved on." He stopped and gave a big sigh. Harry waited. He felt Ole Johnny struggling with his thoughts and didn't want to spoil the moment. They sat there in silence for about ten minutes. Harry didn't mind, believing that Jesus was doing some work in his friend's heart.

Ole Johnny went over to the counter to get more coffee. "More?"

"No thanks, I better get going soon. Can I say a prayer for you before I leave?"

"Yeah, guess so, I probably need lots of prayer."

Harry bowed his head, "Lord Jesus, you know all about me and my friend. You know how we need you. I thank you for your love and care for me all through the years. I thank you for dying for me and for rising from the dead. I pray that my friend would find your peace like you gave me. I commit us to you for this night and this week. Amen."

Ole Johnny wiped a tear from his eye and looked away. "Thanks."

Missing!

HARRY REMEMBERED IT was time for small group meeting they had at the church every Tuesday; it included food. He decided to skip going home and took the bus to the church. Some ladies had brought munchies, but he noticed Leda wasn't there yet. He had talked to her on the phone early that morning. They had prayed for a minute, and he had told her, "See you this evening".

"Hi, Harry. Come sit over here. How's your day been?"

"Hi, thanks. Keepin' busy, but that's good, I like it that way. How about you?"

"Yeah, I've been busy too. Seems like there's no time for the important stuff anymore."

They sat for a few minutes and Harry decided he could trust Jim to talk about Ole Johnny. He shared how he had talked with Johnny and that he had prayed with him. "I'd appreciate if you would pray for him. He's doing a lotta thinking."

"Sure. Do you want the whole group to pray for him or just us two for now?"

"Not the whole group, I'm not used to sharing with a group so much."

Jim prayed a short prayer for Ole Johnny, then it was time to start.

George, the leader of the group talked about trusting Jesus in all situations and about remembering that Jesus is faithful and knows every intricate detail of our lives and cares about our needs. He can be trusted. He is faithful! Many nodded their heads in agreement, including Harry. They prepared to leave. Harry shook Jim's hand and thanked him for his prayers.

On the way home on the bus, Harry wondered about Leda. She was always at small group or if she couldn't make it, she would phone and tell him. He checked his phone but there were no calls. He began to worry something bad happened to her. By the time he got home, he had got himself into a real frenzy. He dialed Leda's number.

Ring...ring...ring... Beep! "leave a message." Harry slammed the phone down and paced the floor. *Where was she? Why didn't she answer the phone? Why wasn't she at small group? She was always there!*

He kept pacing and looking out the window, running his fingers through his hair. He looked at the phone, willing it to ring, but nothing. He sat on his bed and stared at the wall. Thoughts of some tragedy or accident flooded his mind. He was sure something had happened to Leda, he felt it in the center of his being. He had to do something! He didn't know who to call, except Pastor Nick or maybe Betty. Then he told himself he was being silly. Leda was old enough to take care of herself. She didn't need him to rescue her! He spent a sleepless night, tossing and turning. Trying to pray, but nothing would come.

In the morning he was exhausted and depressed. He dragged himself out of bed, ate some breakfast and caught the bus to work.

Steve was waiting for him and took one look, "Are you okay? You look kind of rough. What's happening?"

"Nothin' I'm fine." He turned and got ready to load the forklift with several boxes of paper supplies.

"Wait! I've got another plan for today."

Harry stopped in his tracks and turned around.

"Yeah, we're going to go out on the streets today and give out a bunch of these papers we've been working on."

Harry's stomach was suddenly tense. He wasn't sure he was ready to go out on the streets and hand out papers to whoever was out there.

Steve saw Harry's hesitation. "We need to pray before we go, then we can load these packs into the truck."

Yeah, we better pray hard. I don't wanna do this.

Steve drove down a different street that Harry hadn't seen before. Steve was chattering about how it was going to be a great day and how the Lord was going to work miracles right before their eyes. He stopped by an old run-down apartment building.

"Here we are! I'll bet there's people here that need the Lord." He peered out the window and waited, then he got out and grabbed a few leaflets from the back. "Come on, let's go!"

Harry sat there, not moving. Steve poked his head in the door, "You didn't sign up for this part of the job, did you?" He laughed, kind of making fun of Harry.

Harry felt anger rising, like he'd been tricked. *I can't do this. It's not me, it's not my thing.* He watched Steve walk a few steps and shove a paper at a man shuffling along pushing an old grocery cart loaded with bulging black garbage bags. The anger spilled over, and Harry jumped out of the truck and ran to the old man.

"Leave him alone! He ain't doin' anythin' to bother nobody!" He had a split-second vision of his old self, when he lived on the streets, doing the same thing this old man was doing. He didn't like the memory.

Steve was shocked. "What do you mean? I wasn't hurting him. I was just trying to help him."

"Help him?" Harry shouted. "That's not the way to help him! You know better 'n that! You been there yourself." Harry turned away, clenching his fists and mumbling. Steve backed away from the old man and watched Harry.

Harry jumped back into the truck and slammed the door. He was so angry he couldn't think straight. *Help, Lord!* The Bible verse, "Be still and know that I am God" came into his mind. He took a deep breath and relaxed a little bit. *Thank you, Lord. I know Steve was tryin' to help that guy, but it brought too many memories back to me. I know that YOU are God and that you love that guy out there on the sidewalk, just as much as you love me. And help me to love Steve too.* He sat and felt the peace that only Jesus can give, flood over his body. The tenseness and anger melted away.

He saw Steve talking with the guy in a good way. He wasn't pushing papers in his face or shaking his fist at him. Harry was thankful. He got out of the truck and went over to the two men. He heard the man say something about family. He only caught the end of the conversation but got closer to hear how Steve responded. Steve had his hand on the guy's shoulder and had a loving look on his face. Harry stood still and listened as Steve began praying for the man. His words struck a deep longing in his own heart as he heard Steve pray for the man to find his family.

Harry waited till Steve said "Amen" and then touched the man's shoulder. "Me too. I don't know where my family is either."

The man looked into Harry's eyes and nodded, he didn't need to say anything. Steve waited for a minute, letting the Holy Spirit do His work in both men's lives.

He prayed again, "Lord Jesus, you know the heartaches we all have. You know our deepest longings and needs. Help us to trust you completely and help us to know that you are in control of every part of our lives."

"My name's Harry, what's yours?" Harry asked.

"Bob."

"Nice to meet you, Bob. Is there some way we can help you out? Have you had anythin' to eat? How about we take you to a café?

" Bob's eyes grew big in surprise. "Now, why would you wanna do that? You don't know me. I don't need your help."

Harry remembered how he had refused all the people who had offered to help him over his lifetime. He had run away from them, trying to be independent. Now he knew better, that we are all here to help each other. "I know what you're sayin'. I been there myself. Didn' want nobody to help me till I found out I couldn' do it alone. That's when God sent people along to show me the way back to Him."

Steve chimed in, "Yeah, it was the same with me. I know how it is. Let us give you a ride to the bottle depot at least. It's not far from here."

Bob hesitated for a minute then agreed. He threw his bag in the back of the truck and squeezed into the cab. Bob collected his money for the bottles and was about to take off when Harry stopped him. "We were serious about taking you for something to eat - our treat. Come on, get in."

Bob got back in, but he wasn't too happy about it. Harry knew the craving for alcohol was strong, and especially when a fella had a few dollars in his pocket. He hoped to delay the craving for a few hours by filling Bob's stomach with some food.

Steve turned the truck around and headed back into the main part of town. Harry saw that they were pulling up to the café where Leda worked! Now, if that wasn't God, what was it? But inside the café, Leda did not appear.

A waitress came over to their table. "Morning, how are you?"

Harry's mind was racing. *Where was Leda? She hadn't told him about having a day off. In fact, he hadn't heard from her since yesterday morning.*

"Hi. Haven't seen you before. Have you seen Leda, she's the lady that works here regular."

"Don't know who you're talking about. The manager just called me in because he was short staffed. I used to work here years ago. What'll you have guys?"

Steve took over, "Coffee for me. Bob, what about you?"

Bob mumbled something. Harry spoke up, "He says he'll have the bacon and eggs with coffee. I'll just have an order of toast and coffee."

The waitress turned back to the kitchen. While they waited, a couple of the uppity clan wandered in, making sure they ignored the three sitting by the window. It wasn't long before others came to join them. One was loud and obnoxious. "Hey, Maude, how come you're letting those 'scum' in here. This place is for us. We don't need them bothering us!"

Maude held the coffee pot high and glared at the man. "Do you want coffee or not? It's nothing to you who comes in here. Their money is just as good as yours!" She was about to go back to the kitchen without pouring the coffee.

"If that's the way you are going to be I don't need to be here. Come on fellas. We can find a better place for coffee!" With that, the four men got up and left.

"Sorry about that. Didn't mean to cut some of your business out." Steve said.

Maude shook her head, "I don't need them in here if that's their attitude."

Harry offered a prayer of thanksgiving for the food and for Bob and then said, "Seems there's too many people in this town who have a chip on their shoulder."

"I aim to change that attitude," Steve said.

Bob raised his eyebrows. "Not sure you can do much about that. It's been around for years." He looked down at his plate and stirred the contents like he didn't want anymore.

Harry noticed, "Kinda hard to eat all that when you haven't eaten for a while. It's okay, I remember the feeling. So, where did you sleep last night?"

Bob didn't answer. Harry knew better than to repeat the question. He turned to Steve. "What's you plan for the rest of the day?"

"I think we'll go back to that area where we found Bob, maybe we can put some of our papers in mailboxes."

"Um...I think I'd better go home; I'm not feeling so good. This here Diabetes plays tricks on me, you know?"

Harry paid for his coffee, excused himself and left. All the way home, he worried. He was worried about Leda. It wasn't like her not to call or to not be at work. He was convinced something was wrong. Back at the apartment, he slumped down on the easy chair and heaved a big sigh. He kept checking his cell phone, but there were no calls or messages. He tried calling Leda, but still no answer.

He thought about how much he had grown to care for her. Her kindness and concern about him made him feel loved. Yes, that was it, he loved her. He had been trying to avoid admitting it, but now when he couldn't find her, he knew. He remembered how Leda was concerned about his Diabetes and how she encouraged him to follow his diet and medications. He could almost hear her saying, "Harry, did you check your sugars today? How were they?"

Harry knew it was for his own good, and that she cared, so he reluctantly got up and went over to the cupboard to get the testing machine. He hated poking his finger. He hated this Diabetes that was controlling his life. He hated following a diet. He hated living like this. The only reason he kept at it was to please Leda. If she wasn't around, he would just quit – it was too hard! He glared at the testing machine, turned away and went into the bedroom. He plopped onto the bed and gazed at the ceiling. His thoughts wouldn't stop. His concern about Leda kept swirling around. Maybe he could call the café and ask when she was scheduled to work again. That was it! Maybe they knew. He looked the café number up and dialed. Someone answered, but he didn't know the voice.

"Hi, my name is Harry. I was wondering when Leda Henderson would be in next time."

"And who are you? What's it to you?" the voice growled.

"Don't know. Haven't heard."

The line went dead. Harry's apprehension grew, he felt it in his gut, something was terribly wrong. He decided to call Pastor Nick, but there was no answer. He knew Ron and Betty were at work, no use calling them. He decided to go over to Leda's apartment, maybe someone over there knew where she was.

At the apartment, he rang the buzzer. No response. He kept ringing it, willing her to answer. He got more impatient by the minute. She *had* to be there!

One of the residents came up to the door. "What do you want? Quit being a nuisance!"

Harry glared at her. "I'm lookin' for Leda Henderson. Have you seen her?"

The lady scowled at him, "Nope - not that it's any of your business." She went inside and slammed the door shut.

Harry panicked. *Someone must know where Leda was!* He got on the bus and went back home. He looked at the time. It was mid-afternoon already and he hadn't eaten anything. He didn't care, it didn't matter. All that mattered was to find Leda. He curled up on the bed and fell asleep.

The ringing phone woke him up. He groped around on the bed for the it. "Hello? Hello?" but he was too late, whoever was calling had hung up. He put on his glasses and looked at the call log. It was a strange number with an area code unfamiliar to him. He decided it must be a crank call and threw the phone down in frustration.

He dragged himself into the kitchen and saw the glucose machine sitting on the cupboard. "Oh, well, guess I better check my sugars. Haven't done it for a long time – it's such a bother." When he saw the results on the little screen, he got scared. The reading was 15.6! He hadn't had a reading like that for months! He questioned himself, "Did I take my pills this morning? What did I eat today to make it so high? The machine must be broken. That can't be right!" He threw it down. That evening he tried calling Leda again. Still no answer. Then he called Pastor Nick, but he hadn't heard from Leda either. He agreed it wasn't like her not to contact Harry. Harry tried to stay calm, but his heart was racing. *Something bad had happened to Leda!* He was convinced. Pastor Nick tried to reason with him, but he wasn't listening. He clicked the phone off. The phone rang almost as soon as he put it down. He looked at the call display and saw that it was Pastor Nick. He let it ring several times and picked it up just before it went to the voice mail.

"Harry! Please! Let me pray with you!" Pastor Nick begged. "I understand your concern. It's at times like this that we need to trust in the Lord. He knows where Leda is and He loves her."

Harry listened but didn't say anything.

"Harry! Are you there?"

"Yeah."

The pastor began to pray, saying the words that Harry couldn't. The pain in his heart was too much. Tears rolled down his cheeks. When Nick said 'amen', Harry mumbled a 'thank you' and hung up.

Later, he got a call from Betty, "How's your day going? Haven't heard from you for a while. I see you called today." Then, "How are your sugar levels?"

He admitted that the reading was high, but he figured the machine must be broken. "Maybe I can come over and check it out for you. Can I do that?"

"I 'suppose but don't want to be a bother."

"I'll see you in a few minutes."

Betty helped him do the test again and it showed 18.2 this time. "Harry! That's too high! What's going on? Have you eaten today?" She looked him in the eye and saw he was on the edge of crying. She waited until he could gather his emotions.

"Leda is missing! I haven't heard from her since yesterday morning! We always talk on the phone every evening and even sometimes in the morning before work. Something bad has happened to her! I've got a bad feeling."

"Are you sure? Maybe she went on a holiday or is visiting family."

"I'm sure. She always tells me if she's going away or even calls me when she's not feeling well. I was at the café today and she wasn't there either. They wouldn't tell me nothing. Some new waitress was there."

"Oh, Harry, I'm so sorry."

"I even called Pastor Nick, because he knows a lot of people and I thought maybe he would know where she is. But he didn't." Harry rubbed his eyes and sniffled.

Betty tried to help. "Maybe one of the ladies in your small group would know where Leda went. Do you know who that might be?"

"Naw, I don't have the number of the leader."

"Harry! Listen to me!" Betty reached across the table and patted Harry's hand. "I know why your sugars are so high. Stress can do that you know. You have to try and settle down. I know how much you care for Leda, and I could see that she cares the same about you. Your relationship is beautiful and a gift from God. Remember, God is in control of all things and situations. I know that Leda trusts in the Lord too. Let's pray and ask Jesus to give us wisdom and direction. We need His help!"

Harry bowed his head and felt himself relax as Betty prayed.

"Do you know any of Leda's family?" Betty was searching for some leads. "Do you think we should contact the police? How long is it since you heard from her?"

Harry picked up his phone and flipped through the calls. "She called yesterday mornin', that's the only one from here! Somethin' is wrong!"

"Okay, I'll take you over to her apartment. Maybe the landlord or her neighbours can give us some information."

"I was already there, it's no use."

"Well, maybe if both of us go, we can find something out."

At the apartment, Harry saw a sign posted in a window. It had the manager's number on it. He pointed at it. "Maybe we can call the manager?".

"That's a good idea. I'll try the number." Betty dialed and waited. "Hello? Hi, my name is Betty Matheson, I'm looking for one of your tenants – Leda Henderson. I haven't heard from her. Do you know if she's away or where she is?" Betty heard a big snort.

"How do you think I'd know that? I don't keep track of everyone that lives here. I'm not superman!" Click.

"Let's go up to the door and look at the names. Do you know Leda's number?"

"Yeah, it's coded so you can't see who lives there. It's number 310." They went to the door and pushed the code for 310. It rang and rang, but no answer.

"Harry, it's getting late. I need to work tomorrow. I'll take you home. If you haven't heard anything by morning, maybe you should contact the police?"

Harry walked slowly back to the car. "Yeah."

Stress Levels Going Up

ALL EVENING AND once or twice during the night he kept trying Leda's number. He even called the phone company to see if the calls were going through. They told him the phone was working. The next morning, he tried Leda's phone again. Still nothing. Harry looked at the time. He knew he should let Steve know why he wasn't at work, but he didn't care. He had to find Leda!

He took the bus down to the police station. It had been a while since he'd been in a police station but the memories were still there – most of them bad. He told the front desk lady why he was there and waited while she went to get an officer. The officer came from the back and motioned to follow him into a separate room.

"What seems to be the problem?" His attitude was one of boredom and slightly prejudiced. Harry began carefully. "My girlfriend has disappeared. Her name is Leda Henderson. She always calls me and lets me know if she's going out of town."

"The constable smirked. "Oh yeah, I know. You guys had a fight and she told you to get lost. I've heard it all too many times."

Harry slammed his fist on the table. "We did not have a fight! We get along jus' fine. You don't know anythin'!"

"Calm down! Okay. Tell me when you heard from her last and where she lives."

Harry gave him the information. The constable left the room saying he would be back shortly. Harry began praying real hard. *Lord Jesus! Please help me find Leda. Please make this guy have a little compassion.*

The constable came back after a long time. "We ran a scan on your friend's name, didn't see anything." His attitude seemed to have softened a little.

"Can I file a missing person report?" asked Harry.

"I suppose, but not sure that will get any results. Besides, it's only been three days! We don't have time to start looking for someone that's only been gone three days. Do you know where her family is from?"

"She don' have any family, on her own for a long time."

"Okay, give me your name and number and we'll try and find something out. You can leave now." He showed Harry to the exit and gave him a soft pat on the shoulder.

He waited for the bus and decided he better take the one to Steve's shop. It was no use sitting around his apartment; it was too depressing. Steve was surprised to see him walk in the door. "What's going on? Thought you were sick?"

Harry sat down across from Steve. "It's like this. My girlfriend, Leda, is missing. Haven' heard from her for three days. It's not like her. I got a bad feeling. Somethin's happened to her! I even went to the police this morning. I don't know what to do. I can't think anymore."

Steve sat quietly. "Maybe she went to see her family?"

"She told me her parents died when she was young and she's been on her own for a long time. We were getting' along just fine. The cop tried to tell me we'd had a fight. That made me mad."

"Yeah, that would make me mad too. That's what I mean about this town. There's prejudice everywhere. That's why I'm trying to make a difference. Can you help me look over these pamphlets and tell me what you think about the wording?"

This was the first time Steve had asked Harry for any input. Harry had his own thoughts about the wording but had not said anything. He decided it would be good to think about something else while he waited for the cops to call.

"See, look at this first part of the pamphlet. When you say 'you need Jesus' right at the beginning, it could turn people off. Why not start with, 'have you ever walked beside a homeless man?' or something to grab their attention. Maybe, 'who is your neighbour'? Then put a short Bible verse like 'love your neighbour as yourself'. Then maybe put something about how many people are homeless or living in real needy situations. You have to get them in the gut, you know?"

Steve nodded. "Okay, let's do some fixing on this. Thanks for your thoughts. I guess I had too many negative words and just too many words, period. Nobody will take time to read a whole essay!"

They worked all morning and then decided to take a break. They went over to the café. Harry asked Steve if he could make some inquiries about Leda. Maybe they would treat Steve better. The waitress was new but treated them kindly.

Steve made light conversation with her at first and then said, "By the way, a lady named Leda works here. We had got to know her quite a bit. When will she be in next?"

Harry waited, holding his breath for the answer. The waitress looked at Steve and shrugged. "I don't know. I just started here yesterday. Saw the ad on their website. I can ask the manager though." After a few minutes she came back. "The boss says Leda works here, but she didn't show up, so they got somebody else. Seems she just disappeared."

Harry pushed his half-eaten plate away and hung his head. Steve finished his burger and they left.

"See, I told you somethin' bad has happened!"

By now, Steve was looking quite concerned too. He knew Harry and Leda had been seeing each other a lot, and that they were getting serious. "What if we go down to the police station again. Maybe if I'm with you, they will act a bit differently?" Harry put his hands out as if to say 'whatever'.

The receptionist at the police station nodded and acknowledged Harry. "So you're back. I'll get the constable to see you."

Harry saw the constable's name was Wayne. He showed them into a small room. Wayne was quite reasonable, speaking to Steve more than Harry as they talked about Leda and her disappearance. "We checked the local hospital and contacted some other detachments in the area, but no one has seen your friend's name in their files. Do you have a picture of her?"

Harry dug for his wallet and pulled out a rather worn picture of Leda. "This is a bit old, but she still looks the same. She's got light brown hair, beautiful, sparklin' blue eyes, about my height, but a lot skinnier! She looks much younger than 42, more like late 20s."

"Okay, I'll take a scan of this." He left the room.

"At least he's not just telling you to get lost," Steve remarked. "I think he's really trying to help."

Wayne came back in and handed the picture to Harry. "I'll let you know if we find anything out." With that, he indicated the door.

Back at the shop, Steve and Harry finished the pamphlet and got it re-printed. By then, it was time to close down for the day. "See you tomorrow? Hope they find something out about Leda." Steve patted Harry's shoulder.

Harry pushed himself to go to work the next day, but Leda was always in the back of his mind. He had called her friend Suzie, but she hadn't heard or seen her since last

Sunday. Suzie was worried too. It wasn't like Leda to just take off without telling anyone.

"Did you go to the police?" Harry asked.

"Well, no. I wasn't sure if I should."

Harry was surprised. In his mind, if Suzie was such a good friend she would have been searching too. "Well, I did go to the police an' filed a missin' person report. Maybe if you went and did the same, we could get some answers."

"Yeah, okay, that's a good idea. Talk to you later."

On Saturday, Harry moped around his apartment. Life wasn't worth living. He couldn't get himself into anything. The glucose machine taunted him on the counter until he checked his sugar. Today it was 12.4, still too high. He knew all the stress was having a bad effect on him, but he didn't know how to deal with it. He decided to go and see Ole Johnny, maybe that would help.

Ole Johnny was at home as usual, puttering around the house, now that the yard work was mostly done. "Oh, hello, Harry. Come in. Good to see you!"

Harry sat down at the kitchen table and let Ole Johnny chatter on about getting ready for Thanksgiving. "My missus used to make the best pumpkin pie! Makes my mouth water, just thinking about it. I sure miss her." He stopped and looked at Harry. "Hey! What's up? You look like you lost your best friend."

Harry hung his head and didn't say anything.

"Come on, what's up?"

Harry burst out with, "Have you ever lost a best friend? Then he told Ole Johnny all about Leda and how much he missed her. Ole Johnny nodded, agreeing he knew all about loneliness.

"How about you help me clean up my basement. I've kind of let it go – too many reminders down there. Matilda did lots of sewing, making quilts and stuff. She did beautiful work. Everyone raved about it."

"Sure, I'll help you, got nothin' else to do."

They worked all morning, putting things into piles. One for recycle, one for the second-hand store and one for the garbage. By noon, they were tired and decided to give it up.

"Well, we made a little progress, but there's still lots to do, we'd better take the afternoon off. I heard there was a good movie on downtown. Do you want to go with me? Not much fun going alone, you know."

Harry sat through the show but was having trouble following the story line. Something about a father and son not getting along until the son ran away. At the end, the father changed his ways, and the son came back home.

Ole Johnny dropped Harry off at his apartment. "See you later, thanks for your help." Harry jumped out and waved.

Next day was Sunday and Harry felt the strong urge to go to church. He knew he had been avoiding God and knew that he was mad at God for not answering his prayers about Leda. At church, several people came up to him and said 'hi' and expressed their concern about Leda. It was comforting to know others were missing her too. Then when Pastor Nick prayed, he prayed specifically for Leda. Harry felt a huge burden lifting from his spirit. Just knowing others cared and were praying helped him to feel much better.

Pastor Nick spoke about how God doesn't always answer our prayers when and how we want. Sometimes God is trying to get our attention, to focus on Him more and to trust Him more. Harry felt like he was talking straight to him. *"Yeah, Lord. That's right. I bin avoiding you. Sorry."* At the end of the service Harry went to the front for prayer. A couple of the elders came and prayed with him. One of them, Andrew, asked, "How about if you come to our house for lunch? Ruthie would be glad to have a visitor."

"Are you sure? I don't want to be a bother."

"You're not a bother. We know Leda and are concerned about her too. Ruthie was a good friend."

After lunch, Ruthie talked about how she had met Leda about two years ago, when she came to the church. They had hit it off right away and enjoyed each other's company, going shopping or just having coffee. "She seemed to be very happy the last while, I think it was since she met you, Harry. She talked about you a lot."

Harry averted his eyes and fought to keep the tears from spilling over. "Yeah, we were hitting it off real good. I can't understand why she just left. You know? I got this bad feeling that something terrible has happened to her."

"Yes, me too. I heard that the police put out missing person alert last week."

"Yeah. I went to them and filed the report. I think her friend Suzie did too. Not sure it will do any good."

"But Harry, we have to have faith that the Lord Jesus knows all about this whole situation; that He's in control. I know it's hard to keep having faith, but we have to keep on praying and believing that she will turn up soon."

"Well, I better be getting home. Thanks for the meal, it was great, and thanks for your prayers."

"I'll drive you home."

"Thank you, but that's all right, I need to do some walking - it's good for my health you know."

While he was walking, he noticed Percy's truck approaching. As it got closer, it slowed down and stopped right across from Harry. Percy rolled down the window and yelled, "Hey, Harry! Come over here, I need to talk to you."

Harry wasn't sure he wanted to talk to Percy but he was curious, so he walked across the street.

"Harry, I found out who broke into the yard and now I know it wasn't you. Would you consider coming back to work for me?"

Harry stood by the open window and raised his eyebrows. "You want me back?" A Bible verse came to mind: *'Forgive and you shall be forgiven...'* He thought Percy's offer over. It would be better to work for Percy than Steve. He wasn't too sure where Steve was going with his printing business, and he wasn't too sure he wanted to be there. It was awkward working with Steve as their ideas were often different.

"Yeah, I'd like to come back."

Percy grinned and said, "I'll see you tomorrow morning, usual time." With that he rolled the window up and took off.

Harry stood there, totally stunned. What were the chances of meeting up with Percy on a Sunday afternoon? If he hadn't gone to Andrew and Ruthie's place, he would have missed him. He turned and headed home *Thank you, Lord for getting my job back. I appreciate it!*

At home he saw his pills on the counter and knew he had not taken them. Oh bother! It was so hard to remember everything about this Diabetes 'thing'. Too late to take them today, *I'll try to do better tomorrow.* He dialed Steve's number and left a message about him not coming in anymore and thanked him for his help over the past few weeks. Then he sat down and stared at the wall. *Lord. You know how much I'm missin' Leda. Please take care of her, wherever she is. I put her in your hands.*

A Phone Call

BACK AT THE lumberyard, Percy treated him well, almost bending over backwards trying to make up for his accusations.

At break time Harry asked, "By the way, how did you find out it wasn't me that broke in?"

"The cops did a lot of checking, taking fingerprints, especially on the back door handle. They couldn't find any that belonged to you, so they looked in their files and found they matched some young thugs that have caused lots of trouble in this town."

"You know it was like the Lord was telling me not to touch that door handle. I wanted to go in but resisted the feeling. Sure glad I didn't."

"Yeah, I'm glad too. You're a good worker and I missed you!"

Harry was relieved and glad to hear Percy's comments. It made him feel good. Then he remembered that Percy had laid charges against him, and Ron and Betty had paid for the bail charges.

"Um, Percy there's one thing that needs to get sorted out before we go on. Do you remember that I landed in jail the day of the break-in, and that you laid charges against me?"

"Oh, I had forgotten about that. So, what about it?"

"Well, Ron and Betty paid to get me out and I haven't had the money to pay them back."

Percy was quiet for a few minutes. "Guess I was so mad that I wasn't thinking straight, sorry about your friends having to bail you out. How much did they pay?"

"It was $300.00. Doesn't sound like much but when a guy doesn't have a lot extra to live on, it's a huge amount."

"Thanks for reminding me. I'll make a cheque out, just tell me what name to put on it."

All week, Harry went to work with Percy, but he kept worrying about Leda. Just before the weekend he finally told Percy about Leda being gone. Percy expressed concern and told him he would keep his ears open when he was out and around town.

Every evening Harry checked his sugar levels and saw that they were coming down to normal. He was relieved and knew that he was feeling better. He phoned the police station on Friday afternoon, but they didn't have any new information for him. The non-news made him more depressed. It was two weeks since Leda had disappeared! Again, his gut feeling told him something bad had happened. He called Suzie too, but she didn't have anything to tell him either.

A few minutes later his phone rang, and he saw it was a different area code, one he didn't know at all. He decided to answer it anyway. "Hello? Hello?" He heard a muffled voice trying to tell him something, but he couldn't make out what it was.

"Hello? Who is this? I can't get what you sayin". He held the phone closer. The voice continued to be muffled, but this time he thought he heard, "Harry! Hel..."

"Leda! Is that you? Are you okay? Where are you?" The phone went dead. Harry stared at it in shock. If it really was Leda, he'd have to call the cops. Maybe they could trace the call. He ran to the bus stop, jumped on the bus without paying.

"Hey! You can't ride on here for free! Put your money in the box!"

"Oh, sorry. Here." He showed his pass to the driver. The bus seemed to take forever to get to the police station, stopping at every stop, even if no one was getting on or off. Harry was getting more impatient by the minute. *Lord, help!* He jumped off the bus and almost ran the length of the block to the station. The lady at the reception desk looked bored and irritated when Harry burst through the door.

"Sir! Sir! Please! I don't know what you're talking about! I can't understand what you want. Please calm down."

Harry realized he had been ranting on about Leda because he was so excited. "Sorry. Sorry. I need to talk to a constable. It's about a missing person report."

The lady told him to sit down while she called someone. A young woman in uniform came out. "Sir, my name is Lori, can I help you?" Her manner was somewhat kind but mostly just bored. She led Harry to a separate room and again asked if she could help him.

He told her that Leda Henderson was on the missing persons list and that he had received a phone call that sounded like it might be her. He showed her the call display number and asked if she could trace it. She wrote the number down and left the room. Harry silently prayed that this one number would be a break-through. The minutes ticked by agonizingly slow. He stood up and paced around the room. There were no windows and nothing on the walls, nothing to take his mind off the waiting. The constable came back, along with another member. Harry didn't like the look on their faces. He forced himself to sit on the chair.

"What is your name, sir, and how are you related to this case?"

"My name is Harry Bearpaw, and I filed a missing person report two weeks ago. Leda is my girlfriend. We were very close. I miss her so much." He managed to keep his emotions controlled.

"Okay, I see. This is Constable Jeffery. He was checking the number on your phone. It turns out it's in Toronto! We have to do more checking because there was no name connected with it. When we tried to call the number there was no answer. We will be contacting the police in Toronto for their assistance. What did the voice say when you took the call?"

"It was so muffled I couldn't make out much, except the voice called me by name and started to say something else, but then the phone went dead. I know it was Leda. How could somebody know my name way over there?"

"Okay, Harry, we will keep following up on this, but for now you can go home. We will call if we find anything out." The constables stood up. Harry knew the interview was over and reluctantly walked out.

He caught the bus home and made himself some supper. Then he called Suzie and told her about the call. She got all excited too and said she would call Pastor Nick to put a request out on the prayer line.

Harry didn't sleep much that night. He kept hearing the voice on the phone and it tore his heart out. He felt so helpless and alone. *Here I am again Lord. This is way bigger than anythin' I've ever had to handle. Please, take care of Leda. Please bring her back to me. Please!*

The next morning on the way to work he got a call from Pastor Nick, reassuring him that people were praying and that God was in control of where Leda was and what was happening to her. Harry thanked him and felt a little better.

He told Percy about the call and admitted he might not be working as well as usual, with so much on his mind.

Percy seemed to be extra kind that day and several times allowed Harry to be alone. Harry willed his phone to ring, but nothing came. He was tempted to call the police station but decided he'd better not 'bug' them too much. He hoped they were working on the case. In the evening he got a call from Betty inquiring if he had heard anything and about how he was doing with his sugar levels. He told her the levels had been going well since he was working for Percy, but this phone call had set everything off again.

"Harry, keep taking your pills and don't forget to eat! You have to keep your energy up. I'm sure you will hear something soon. Keep praying – we are!"

By Wednesday, he had heard nothing from the police. He asked Percy if he could leave early, so he could stop by the police station and Percy agreed. At the station, the receptionist received him with a slight smile of recognition and said she would get someone to talk to him. This time it was Wayne, the first constable he had spoken with. In the side room, Wayne pulled some papers out of a file folder and laid them on the table. "This is what we have so far. The phone number is in Toronto. As you know, Toronto is a huge city and the police department there is very busy. We had lots of trouble even getting them to respond to our calls. Just today, we got to talk to them. It's good you came in. We were going to call you soon."

"Well, what do you know? Please! This is driving me crazy!" Harry's agitation was growing. He was tempted to stand up and demand information from this guy who sat calmly at the desk.

"Harry, we're trying to do our best. Please listen to me. The Toronto police tell us the number is located in a certain district that is not the best. They said they will look into it more but seemed like they were in no hurry to help us out. There's nothing more we can do from this end, except wait."

Harry felt a huge load of depression fall on his spirit. He sat for a long time as Wayne waited.

"Thank you. I know you're trying to do your job, but it's hard. I've got lots of people praying for Leda. I have to keep believing that the Lord will take care of her. Thanks."

Wayne nodded and stood up, shook Harry's hand and showed him to the door.

That evening, Harry remembered it was small group night at the church. He felt like maybe he could get some support from the group, so he got ready and went. Bob welcomed him warmly and asked immediately if there was any news about Leda. Harry shared with the group what he had heard that day.

Bob said, "Let's pray".

Harry felt peace settle over him as he heard several of the group voice their concerns for Leda and ask the Lord to protect her and bring her home safely. During the Bible study time, Bob read from Phil. 4:6 *"Be anxious for nothing, but in everything by prayer and supplication, with thanksgiving, let your requests be made known to God."* He emphasized the part of the verse about being thankful.

"We are so thankful to the Lord that we have heard from Leda. That is a huge thing to be thankful for!" Then he talked about not being anxious, that was the hard part. Our natural tendency is to worry and fret and get impatient. But God is in control, and He will work everything out in His time.

Harry was glad he had gone to the group. He felt encouraged by the Bible verses and by the prayers of many. He slept better that night.

Sunday rolled around and Harry looked forward to church. He appreciated the support he felt from those who knew Leda. Even though he hadn't heard anything from the police, he was at peace, trusting in the Lord to work things out in His time.

After the service he noticed a single man standing in the foyer who had been at church recently. Harry wanted to help him feel at ease with everyone, so he walked over.

"Hi, my name's Harry."

The man looked down and was quiet.

Harry tried again. "So, do you live near here?"

This time the man answered belligerently. "No, I live clear on the other side of town. I need to get back home." and turned to leave.

"Wait! I was going to ask you to go for lunch with me. I'd be glad to have some company, gets kind of lonesome sometimes. What did you say your name was?"

"I didn't say." Then he mumbled. "Wally."

"Hi, glad to meet you, Wally. How about lunch? I'll buy. The Lord has provided me with a job, so I want to share with you."

"Well, I suppose I can take you up on the offer. Doesn't need to be a fancy lunch."

On the bus, Harry made a couple of efforts at making conversation, but Wally was quiet. At the café Harry reminded Wally that the dinner was on him and told him to order whatever he wanted. Maude the waitress, recognized Harry and immediately asked about Leda. Harry shook his head, "nothing".

Wally looked up in surprise. "How do you know Leda?"

It was Harry's turn to be surprised. He was almost speechless. "I've been friends with Leda for several months, but she disappeared three or four weeks ago. Do you know her?"

Wally fumbled with the knife and fork, moving them back and forth. Harry waited.

"It's like this. I met Leda about two years ago. She's a very special lady. I thought we were getting along fine, but all of a sudden she quit talking to me. Couldn't figure it out. Then I heard she went to the church we were at this morning so I figured I'd see if I could find her again."

A thousand ideas flew through Harry's mind. *Had Leda 'stood' this guy up? Had she 'stood' him up too? How could this be?*

"What do you mean getting along fine? Was she your girlfriend?" Harry had to know. All his feelings about Leda were beginning to crash around him. *Had she been leadin' him on, trickin' him into thinkin' she cared for him?*

"Yeah, guess you'd call it that. We were getting pretty serious."

Their order arrived and Harry prayed for the food and then tried to eat. He was so confused. Wally ate silently too. When the waitress brought the bill Harry paid and they prepared to leave. "Which bus do you take?" Wally said the number.

"Mine goes the opposite way. Guess I'll see you around sometime." He still was in so much shock he couldn't think of anything more to say.

"Yeah, see you later." Wally turned and walked away.

All afternoon, Harry wrestled with what Wally had said. He couldn't believe it. Leda wasn't that kind of woman. She wasn't sneaky and underhanded. Wally must have been lying, just trying to cause trouble or something. He decided to call Pastor Nick and ask him if he knew Leda before Harry knew her.

Harry accepted Pastor Nick's invitation to meet him for coffee at the church. There was a small group meeting so he knew the place would be open.

Harry questioned him about Leda, like, how long had she been coming to the church? Then, do you know this guy named Wally?"

The pastor tried to get Harry to settle down. He saw Harry shifting his weight around on the chair every few minutes and running his hands through his hair.

"Harry, please listen to me. Leda is a fine woman, as honest as I've ever seen. I've met lots of people over the years and God shows me when people are giving me a story that doesn't add up. She's not like that, she's the 'real deal'. Her faith is strong. I have the feeling that Wally wasn't telling you the whole story. I don't know who he is, but if he was at church just to find Leda, then maybe he needs the Lord, not Leda. Harry, the Lord knows all about this turn of events and He knows where Leda is. Sometimes it feels like God isn't listening. Look here in Psalm 13. It says, 'How long Lord? How long will you turn your face from me?' This is one of those times when we're asking, 'how long'? We need to pray for extra patience and extra faith and trust."

Harry knew what Pastor was saying was true, but he struggled with fully trusting in this situation. He left for his apartment, trying to pray, but his mind was still in a turmoil. Next day, he worked hard, only taking short breaks. He needed to keep busy, to keep his mind off things. Percy was quite obliging, pleased that Harry was working and accomplishing so much.

Harry went back to the small group and felt much better being with the new friends he was making. Their ongoing prayers reassured him that Jesus was listening and really did care. By Friday, Harry decided to make another visit to the police station. He knew if he didn't keep pestering them, the file could get lost in all the paperwork.

At the police station he met with Wayne again. "Let me get the file to refresh my memory." Wayne came back and plopped a bulging file on the table. "Looks like someone has been doing some investigating since we last talked." He shuffled the papers, scanning them quickly. He stopped at one and stared. "Whoa! What's this?" Harry's heart jumped!

"I see here that your lady friend was contacted on the third – that's a week ago! I don't understand why you weren't notified." Wayne frowned.

"Where was she? Who talked to her, why......?"

"I don't understand this. Let me check with the person that wrote this report." He left abruptly. Harry stood up and paced. He prayed and paced and prayed.

Wayne came back at last. "Please sit down. Let me show you this report." He started at the top, with the time and date, then went past some unimportant notes. He turned to the next page and thrust it across the table. "Look here. It says Leda Henderson was located in a motel in a small town near Toronto. The investigating officer talked directly to her. She said she was fine. She didn't want anyone to look for her, to just leave her alone."

"I don't believe it!" Harry leapt to his feet and pounded the desk. "It's not true! Leda isn't like that! There's something wrong!"

"Please, sir! I've only told you what was found."

"Where's this person that talked to the investigating officer? I have to talk to him. Now! I'm not leaving till I talk to him!"

Wayne could see that Harry wasn't simply going to go away. "I'll see if I can find him."

An older officer came into the room and held his hand out to Harry. Harry didn't respond.

"Who are you? When did you talk to Leda? Why didn't you call me? What kind of cop are you?"

"Sir, you must understand we have lots of missing person files and it gets very difficult to keep on top of everything. My name is Monty and I apologize for not calling you. I forgot."

"Forgot!! That's no excuse! Is Leda just another number in your file system?"

"Please sit down!" Monty put his hand on Harry's shoulder, but Harry flinched and turned away. He was trying desperately to get control. He faced the wall, with his back to the two men. *Help, Lord! Help!* "Okay, I'll try to calm down." He sat on the chair and looked the officer in the eye. "Tell me."

Monty leaned across the table a bit, holding the file in his hands. "It's like this, sir. I put many calls into the police department in Toronto before I even got someone who would talk to me. They traced the number you gave us to a small town outside the city. When they called it, there was no answer, so they dispatched a local officer to check into it further. It turned out to be a motel number. The officer went to the motel and inquired if Leda Henderson was registered there. At first they told him no one by that name was there, but on further questioning, admitted that they had heard her name mentioned by another guest. The officer demanded that he be allowed to speak with Leda, so they relented at last and showed him to the room. The manager knocked on the door but there was no answer. He used his master key to gain entry.

There was a woman asleep on one bed and a second one jumped up when the door opened. Of course, seeing the police in the room caused a lot of panic. It took a few minutes to calm the women down, but when they asked if Leda Henderson was there, one looked shocked, but denied it. The constable kept asking if they were okay and they kept insisting they were fine, but they weren't very convincing. There was nothing else the police could do except to let them know someone was concerned about a woman named Leda Henderson. That's all I have to tell you, I'm sorry."

Harry's mind whirled. "What about the call I got from that number - that called me by name and was asking for help before the line went dead?"

"I don't know. I can't answer that. There's nothing more we can do. Please excuse us." Both men ushered Harry to the front reception and went back to their offices.

Losing Hope

HARRY SPENT ANOTHER restless night. In the morning he phoned Betty and asked if he could come over. It just so happened that they were planning on being home all day and welcomed his visit. Over a cup of coffee, Harry told them the whole story about Leda and Wally and the cops. Ron and Betty offered some suggestions but were at a loss about the situation.

Harry sat in silence, mulling the problem over. "Do you think we could hire a private 'eye' or somebody to search for her?"

Ron immediately said, "Do you know how much that would cost? It would be completely out of reach!"

"Yeah, I know. Just grasping at straws."

Betty reached across the table and put her hand on Harry's arm, "You know, there are some situations in our lives when we come to a roadblock. Sometimes it's God that puts the block there, but sometimes it's our enemy, Satan, trying to discourage and condemn us. I don't know which it is, but I do know that God is in control of every part of our lives, and He loves us more than we can ever know. We have to trust Jesus even when nothing makes sense. Can you put Leda and everything that's connected to her into God's hand and leave it there?"

Harry sat with his head bowed, snuffling every so often. He was quiet for a long time. He pulled his arm away from Betty's touch, pushed the chair away from the table and stood up. He still didn't say anything, just stared at Ron and Betty. They didn't try to stop him. They knew he needed to sort things out in his own time.

"See you, Harry. We're praying for you."

Christmas Banquet

WEEKS WENT BY. Harry did his best to put everything into the hands of Jesus, but thoughts of doubt and worry were not far from his mind. He continued to attend church and small group, finding some comfort in being with other Christians. One of the guys, Richard, began to talk to him more and soon they became friends. Richard was just the best kind of guy for Harry. When Harry shared his doubts and worries, Richard would take his Bible and show him a verse that was just right for a situation. Harry began to understand how he could hold onto the promises throughout the day, pulling it up in his memory when doubts taunted him. As a result, his faith began to grow. He was able to tell the others in the small group how Jesus had helped at work or when he was riding the bus.

"I'm learnin' that Jesus really cares about every little thing in my life. I used to think that He should be called only when I had a big problem, 'cause I thought I could tend to the little things on my own, but Jesus wants us to depend on Him every minute of every day."

"Preach it, bro!" A man on the other side of the circle smiled and raised his hand with a thumbs up sign. Harry was encouraged and knew the path he was choosing to walk was exactly what the Lord wanted him to do.

He didn't consider himself a preacher at all, but it felt like when he spoke up people listened. *Lord, what do you want me to do with my life? Where do you want me to go?* It didn't mean he had abandoned all hope of ever seeing Leda again; he continued to pray and trust the Lord for her safe return, but he needed to look to the future.

Christmas season was nearing, and the church was preparing for a banquet to be given for those who were alone or who couldn't afford to have a dinner with all the trimmings. Harry joined in and offered to help distribute flyers to the one area of the city that was familiar to him. He especially wanted to find Ally and invite him to the banquet.

All that week, Harry handed out flyers. He stopped to see Ole Johnny too. They had a great visit and Ole Johnny said he'd like to come. He asked Percy too, even though he knew Percy wasn't poor or homeless. Harry hoped the Christmas message would give Percy something to think about besides his business.

Missing Leda almost became an obsession. He tried to put it in God's hand and tried really hard to keep trusting, but he was getting impatient. Why didn't God answer his prayers and the prayers of many others? In fact, he was getting downright angry with God - again! He knew it wasn't right, but he couldn't help it. Patience wasn't one of his strong points. Ron and Betty and Richard kept reassuring him that God would answer at the right time, but that God's answer isn't always what we want to hear.

The evening of the Christmas banquet arrived. Harry was at the door, welcoming people. He saw some dressed real fancy and others had thread-bare jeans and jackets that didn't keep them warm in the frigid air. Harry directed the visitors to another helper who ushered them to a table. Eyes sparkled when they saw the beautiful decorations. Red streamers and white balloons hung from a central light. The tables had fine white tablecloths and candle centerpieces. One person from the church was sitting at each table to welcome the guests. Harry was almost ready to leave his station at the door when he spied Steve hanging around outside. It looked like he was trying to make up his mind about coming in.

Harry opened the door, "Hey, Steve! Come on in! I'm glad to see you."

"Oh, I was just wandering by, I'm not dressed up enough to go in there!"

"It don't matter how you're dressed, just come in!" Reluctantly, Steve agreed, and Harry walked with him to a table, noticing that Ally was sitting with Richard at another table. Harry was pleased.

The meal was superb. A full turkey dinner was brought to each one at the table. The music and story after the meal was brief but gave a clear message of what Christmas was about. Pastor Nick emphasized the fact that Jesus was born in a barn and was from a poor family. "We don't have to be rich and have a comfortable house to know Jesus. He comes to us right where we are, and He knows our situation because He's been there Himself." A short prayer was said and then the group was dismissed.

Harry tried to make conversation with Steve but didn't have much luck. Later, he went over to Ally and asked him how he liked the banquet. "Good!" was all the response he got. Afterwards, the men and women of the church cleaned up the tables, dishes, and floors before leaving for the night. Just before they were ready to leave, Pastor Nick gathered the group and prayed for each person who had come. He prayed that they would know the love of Jesus in their lives in spite of their difficulties. At the end, he even prayed for Leda to come home for Christmas! Harry was shocked. It was almost like a sign. Like Nick knew something that Harry didn't. He didn't have a chance to ask

Nick why he prayed like that; too many people were around him.

Ron and Betty gave him a ride to his apartment. He prepared for bed and began reading his Bible, but he was too tired and fell asleep. He dreamt that Leda had come back but the dream ended abruptly when he woke up in a cold sweat. Was he having a nightmare? Was Leda really coming back? He couldn't sleep much the rest of the night.

A Christmas Miracle!

"HARRY! HARRY!" THE voice on the phone was urgent. "Harry! Where are you?"

Harry looked at the clock, it was 6:30 am. He heard Leda's voice yelling at him. Was he still dreaming? He listened again.

"Harry! Answer me!"

"Leda is that you? For sure is that you? I love you! I've missed you so much! Where are you?" He waited, holding his breath. Could it really be Leda?

"Harry! I love you! I've missed you too. Listen to me! I need you to come and get me! There's no bus service here."

"But, where are you? I don't have a car. How can I come and get you?"

"Harry! God has made it possible for me to escape from the guys that took me. I made it back to Winnipeg. God did a miracle! I'm at Everton, that's in southern Manitoba. Can you get someone to bring you here to get me? The only ones who care about me are you and the church family. Please! Help me!"

"Wait! I'll call Richard and see if he can help. Can I get back to you at this number? Is this a cell phone or what?"

"Yes, that's another miracle! I've only got a few minutes on it. I'll tell you all about it when you come. Love you! Bye."

Harry was so excited he had trouble remembering Richard's number. "Richard! Guess what? Leda just called me! She's in Everton, MB. I think that's about four hours from here. She needs me to come and get her."

"You got a call from Leda? Really? Praise God!" Richard was astounded. "I can't take you, but I'll call around and see if anyone is free to drive over there. It's pretty early in the morning, but I'll get back to you." Richard hung up.

Harry sat staring into space. He could hardly believe that Leda had called. Maybe he was still dreaming. His phone rang and he saw it was Richard. "I'm having trouble finding anyone that isn't already tied up with other things. It's always so busy right before Christmas. I'll keep trying."

"Maybe I'll call Betty. Maybe she knows someone. Thanks." He left a message on Betty's phone and then thought about Percy. *Lord is that you speakin'? Why would Percy be willin' to help me out? I need to know that it's really You tellin' me to call Percy.*

He waited for a couple of hours and hadn't heard from Richard or Betty. He was getting discouraged and began worrying. *What if I can't find anyone to help Leda out? What would happen to her? I can't let her down.* He had to do something! Again, the thought came to him about Percy. He knew Percy wasn't busy on Saturdays. He didn't have a family and the business was closed.

"Hi, Percy! How are you doin'?" He listened as Percy rambled on about some guy that owed him money. Harry got up enough courage to get down to why he was calling. "Percy, you know I been worryin' about my girlfriend, right?"

Percy, "Yeah, so?"

Harry told him about the phone call and how she was needing someone to come and get her. "Would you be willin' to take me over to Everton, MB to bring her home? I know it's a lot to ask. You can take the gas money out of my wages, and besides, I've got a little extra to pay you." There was a long silence at the other end of the phone. Harry managed to keep his mouth shut and wait.

"Harry, do you know how long it takes to drive to Everton? It's at least four hours and then four hours back, that's a long day!"

"I know, I know. But this is an emergency. I don't know who else to call. Everybody is too busy."

"Let me think about this for a bit. I'll get back to you." The phone went dead. Harry waited. And waited. The time was ticking so slowly, he could almost count every time the hand moved on his little alarm clock. It was already 8:00 in the morning. Harry jumped when the phone finally rang. "Hello?"

"Yeah, I've been thinking about the trip to get your girlfriend. I guess I can take you there. When do you want to leave?"

"You will? Really?" Harry held his breath. He couldn't believe what he was hearing. "Could we leave by 9? Does that give you time to get ready?"

Harry dialed the number Leda had given him. "Hi, Leda, guess what? Percy is going to drive me over to where you are. I'm so thankful!" Leda gave a short answer and hung up.

To The Rescue!

THE WEATHER WAS clear and cold, and roads were dry. They headed east, driving into the bright morning sun. Percy drove intently, like he was having trouble seeing the road. Harry managed to keep quiet and to wait until Percy was ready to talk. If they had to drive in silence the whole way, Harry decided he would have to do it. About halfway, Percy slowed down and pulled into a service station. "Guess we better take a break and fill up."

"I'll put the gas in like I promised." Harry jumped out and hurried to the gas pump. When he was finished, he went in to get a coffee and snack. Back on the road, Percy continued to drive in silence. Harry kept his mind busy, recalling scripture verses and marveling at the beautiful landscape unrolling before them. He couldn't stand it any longer and decided he had to say *something*.

"Percy, I sure 'ppreciate you takin' the time to drive me over here. God bless you for doing it!" Percy remained silent. He waited a while and tried again. "You know, I had almost given up ever hearin' from Leda again. She's been gone three months. The people in my church kept tellin' me to keep prayin' and to keep trustin' the Lord, but I was really having a lot of trouble having any faith this last while. I was gettin' mad and impatient with God. God wasn't doing anythin' – at least that's what it felt like. I almost was givin' up on prayin' anymore, like there was a solid glass ceilin' between me and God."

All of sudden he felt a nudge in his spirit to stop talking. *Okay, Lord. I'll let you do the talking to Percy.* When they were nearing their destination, Harry pulled out his phone and dialed Leda's number. It rang for a lot of rings and Harry almost shut it off.

"Hello? Hello?" Harry's heart leapt and he grasped the phone tightly. "Hi, honey. Percy and I will be there soon. Where can we find you?" He repeated the directions out loud as she gave them to him so Percy could hear them too. "Hang on, we'll be there soon." Harry pulled out a scrap of paper and wrote what he could remember of the directions.

They drove into the small town and looked for the landmarks Leda had given. Sure enough, her directions were good, and they pulled up in front of a small motel. Harry could hardly wait for the truck to stop and jumped out. He saw Leda standing outside the motel room. She looked different, her beautiful brown hair was clipped so short it was almost not there, but her blue eyes were the same – sparkling and smiling at him. She ran toward him and they hugged each other, weeping and whispering, "I love you, I love you!"

Harry kissed her full on the lips and electric shocks ran down his spine as she responded to him. He didn't want to let go of her, but he heard a beep from the truck horn. *Oh yeah, Percy was waiting.* He tore himself apart from Leda and held her at arm's length searching her face. Searching to see if she had been hurt in any way.

"Harry! Stop! Let me get my few things out of the room. Your friend is in a hurry." She ran back into the motel room and came out with a small sports bag. "I'll go and return the key. I'll be right back."

"Do you need money to pay for the room?" Harry was following her to the motel office. Leda shook her head and left him lagging behind.

"Okay, I'm ready, let's go. I can't talk right now. I'll tell you all about how God worked a huge miracle for me as we drive."

Harry and Leda sat in the back seat of Percy's truck. Percy had hardly uttered a word to Leda or to Harry when they climbed in the back.

"Percy, when we get on the road for about an hour, let's stop for something to eat. You need a break I'm sure."

Leda began telling them about what had happened to her.

"I had talked to you Harry that morning, right? I was planning to go to the small group in the evening, so I stopped by the store to get some snacks. I was the only one waiting for the bus, then a guy came along and started making small talk. I recognized him from the café, because he often came in for lunch. He had always been friendly and respectful. The bus was late for some reason and all of a sudden, a black car with dark windows pulled up to the curb. I wasn't paying much attention at first, but then this 'nice guy' turned into a monster. He grabbed me from behind, put his hand over my mouth and shoved me into the back seat of the car and climbed in beside me. He was so strong I didn't have a chance. A tough looking guy with long blonde hair sticking out from under an old ragged cap was the driver. He gunned the car and we sped off. I began asking where he was taking me and why. I was shivering from shock and cold. The 'nice' gentleman growled at me to shut up or I would get what was coming to me and tied a blindfold over my eyes. My mind was in a giant turmoil, I couldn't think. I couldn't even pray. I was in so much shock. We drove for hours. It was dark and I had no idea where we were. They only stopped for pit stops and some 'to-go' snacks. When I went into the washroom the 'nice' guy stood at the door until I came out. They had taken my purse away and wouldn't let me have it even in the washroom. I heard the driver call the 'nice' guy "Joe". I begged Joe to let me go. He just laughed with an evil sneer. "Lady we'll let you out when and where we decide, not when you want out." Sometime during the night, I fell asleep from sheer exhaustion and hunger.

The next day a new driver appeared, and we kept going. It was unbelievable. Whenever I asked for the bathroom, they would say I could wait and kept on. The second night they finally stopped. By then they had taken the blindfold off and I could see the glow of city lights but couldn't see any signs to tell me where we were. I was taken into a motel room, where I met another woman. She was skinny and bedraggled, with a tight, revealing dress hugging her body. She barely acknowledged me when I was thrust into the room. The door clicked behind me, and I heard another lock being slid into the jamb. It was then that I cried out to God with all my might. I cried, "Jesus! Jesus! Help me! Help me!" as I lay on the bed and sobbed." Leda took a deep breath and stopped talking, as if the memory was too terrible to recall.

Percy pulled into a café and told them they were going to have something to eat. Before they ate, Harry prayed a heartfelt prayer of thanks for Leda's return and for the food and especially for Percy. Harry got excited as he told her about the Christmas banquet and about the care group. Percy concentrated on his plate. After the meal they headed out. Leda was fast asleep within minutes, nestled against Harry's shoulder. He kept saying to himself, *Thank you Lord! Thank you, Lord!* He was so full of thankfulness he couldn't think of any other words to say right then.

Hours later they were coming into familiar territory. Harry squeezed Leda and urged her to wake up. "We're almost home! Look! There's the service station just outside of town. Did you have a good rest?"

Leda rubbed her eyes and sat up, pressing the wrinkles out of her long skirt. She pulled her light summer jacket closer and shivered.

Harry dialed Pastor Nick. "Guess what? We've got Leda! We're almost home, can we come to your place? Okay, we'll be there soon. Thanks!"

Pastor Nick and Rhonda met them at the curb when they arrived. Rhonda pulled the truck door open and grabbed Leda, giving her a bear hug. They both shed tears of joy as they embraced.

Nick went around to the driver's side and opened the door. He shook Percy's hand. "God bless you! Thank you so much for helping Harry bring Leda home. It truly is a Christmas miracle! God will reward you for your kindness."

Percy held his hands in an open gesture, "Naw, it wasn't that much." He looked in the back seat to see if Harry had taken everything out.

Harry ran around to thank Percy. "Thank you! Thank you! I don' know how to ever repay you for your kindness. How much do I owe you for gas and you time?"

Percy shrugged, "It was nothing." He took the cash Harry offered and said, "Got to get going. See you later."

"Let's go inside, it's too cold to stand around." Nick led the way to the back door.

Inside, Rhonda scurried around the kitchen to put the coffee on. She saw that Leda was shivering. "Here, let me wrap this fleece blanket around you. You've been through a lot. We can take care of you. We're just so thankful that the Lord brought you back to us." Leda snuggled into the blanket and stared into space.

"Are you okay, Leda?" Rhonda put her arm around her. "Can you talk about it, or maybe later."

Leda nodded, 'Yeah, later. I'm still in shock."

Nick and Harry came into the kitchen. They had been talking in the living room, where Harry told the part of Leda's story she had shared. They also talked about where she was going to live. Suzie, Leda's friend, had told them the apartment manager put all of Leda's stuff out on the street because she hadn't paid her rent. The care group from church went and picked it up and stored it in a friend's basement.

As they drank their coffee and ate a fresh cinnamon bun, Harry sat with his arm around Leda helping to warm her up. Leda seemed to be unable to express her thoughts, she just kept looking down and avoiding everyone's eyes.

"Leda, I feel that you've been through a great deal of trauma and stress the last three months. Sometimes it's good to talk about it. When we know what you've been through, we can know how to help you better." Pastor Nick extended his hand to pat Leda's arm. Tears began to trickle down Leda's cheeks and she began to sob uncontrollably. Harry held her tightly, stroking her shorn head.

"It's okay, honey. We can wait."

Rhonda cleared the dishes and suggested they go into the living room. Leda laid her head on Harry's shoulder as they sat on the couch. She took a deep breath.

"I ... I ... don't know where to start. I just want to forget the whole thing and get back to normal."

Nick nodded, "I understand, but the wounds can only begin to heal when you clean out all the putrid poison that's in there."

Leda sat and thought about that for a minute. "Yes, you're probably right. But I'm not sure if I want Harry to hear all the gory details." She turned to look at him.

"Honey, I can handle it, remember? I've been around the 'block' a few times in my life."

With another big sigh, she began to tell them what happened once they got to the motel. She had learned from the other woman in the motel room that they were near Toronto. She could hardly believe she had been brought so far from home. The other woman's name was Jodie. Jodie told her about the guys who had brought her there. The details shook Leda to the core. They were running a human trafficking ring, using women they captured for their brothels. Leda said she had broken out in tears and began pleading with God to rescue her. She prayed like she'd never prayed before in her life. Jodie had sat on the bed listening to Leda's prayers but didn't offer much encouragement.

She told her, "They will use you where they want, and your God isn't going to rescue you. I've been praying for months and nothing good has happened, just more and more bad." Then she had pulled the blanket over her head, indicating the subject was closed.

Leda went on to tell how the men had brought her some clothes, shoes, makeup, and toiletries with instructions to get dressed and be ready for 'work'. Jodie had laughed at how naïve Leda was. She told her she would soon learn the 'ropes'.

Leda paused and shuddered again. Harry continued to hug her close and reassure her. "I can't tell you the rest, it's too horrible! I'm sure you can fill in the blanks."

Rhonda was sitting on the other side of Leda. "That's okay. Tell us how you escaped. We have been praying that you could be home for Christmas. It truly is a miracle! We are so thankful!"

"Yes, that part of the ordeal is something I can talk about. I was careful to watch where they took me each night, noticing where the bus stops were and where there was a mall or big store. Of course, they always had a man watching me like a hawk, threatening me over and over if I tried anything. I kept praying and begging God to help me, even though Jodie taunted me and told me praying was useless. One good thing that came out of this whole mess is that Jodie began to listen to me when I talked about Jesus. I shared with her how much He loved her and told her the Good News of the Gospel. She gradually began to listen, and I prayed she would understand and accept it. Believe it or not, we found a Gideon Bible in the motel room! How cool is that? I showed her the scriptures right from the Word and I noticed she was reading it when she thought I wasn't looking. Jodie accepted Jesus just a couple of weeks ago. We prayed that Jesus would help us find a way of escape.

Between us we started to make a plan. We knew there was a man watching our motel room at all times, so the only time we could make a break for it was when we were at 'work'. Jodie was in a different building than I was but kept alert for any cracks in our captivity. One day Jodie told me she had seen another woman in her building who was also making plans to escape. They had a few very brief talks and Jodie shared with her what they were planning.

One morning we prayed, begging God to rescue us, then we put the whole thing into His hands and left it there. That night, Jodie made an excuse to her 'guard man'. She told him she needed some 'supplies' from me and without much argument, he let her come to see me. That was the first miracle! When she knocked on my door, I left the guy on the bed, sound asleep (another miracle!). We took off down the back stairs of the building and ran down the alley, pretty sure no one had followed us. I remembered there was a big store at the end of the alley and we ran in there. We searched for a security guard or a manager. All the while we were praying for the Lord to help us find the right person who would help us.

On the third floor we saw a female security guard in a uniform. We felt like maybe she was safe to approach.

We managed to get her in a private corner and tell her our story. She seemed not to believe us at first, but as we told her more, she began to nod and make some notes on her phone. Then she took us down a back stairwell to the main office of the store. That's when I had the chance to call you, Harry. They let me use their phone for a minute. Jodie was also allowed to call her family. The police came and took us to the station to make a statement. That was another miracle! We met a Christian cop! Can you believe it? She was so kind. She referred us to a women's shelter and made some calls to a social worker who dealt with situations like ours. Within a few hours we were given some new clothes (like this skirt and jacket), and some money to get us home on the train. Jodie lives in a small town in Ontario, so she got off and I kept going. We went our separate ways but promised to keep in touch. That reminds me, I need to call Jodie and see if she made it home too."

Pastor Nick, Rhonda and Harry were so entranced by her story, they just sat there. Finally, Nick came to his senses and went to get the portable phone. Leda dug through her purse and found the paper she was looking for and dialed Jodie's number. "Hi Jodie! This is Leda. Did you make it home? Are you okay?" She listened intently and a big smile broke out. "Praise God! Praise God! I'm safe and sound with Harry and our pastor. I'm so thankful we had each other through that terrible ordeal." She chattered on while Harry excused himself for a few minutes.

His mind was reeling. He thought about how his dear Leda had been abused and it made him so angry he could hardly contain it.

Nick came into the kitchen and saw Harry's red face and clenched fists. "Harry, I know her story is terrible, but it's over. She is home and safe. God was truly in control, even in the darkest hour. Jesus didn't leave her, and He hasn't left us either." He put his arm around Harry's shoulder. "We need to call Suzie and tell her the good news; she will be anxious to see Leda too."

They could hear Rhonda talking quietly to Leda in the other room and decided it was best if they stayed away for a while. Harry pulled out his cell phone and dialed Suzie to tell her where Leda was. "Oh! Praise God! I'll be over in a few minutes. I can't wait to see Leda. I'm so thankful she's safe. She can stay at my place tonight."

The next day was Sunday and Pastor Nick set aside the main portion of the service for praise and worship, in thankfulness for Leda's safe return. Leda was unable to say much, she was overwhelmed at all the love being poured out on her.. She just rested in the presence of Jesus and nestled against Harry's shoulder.

After the service many people gathered around Leda to give her hugs and words of encouragement. Harry reluctantly stood back and waited.

Christmas Celebration

HARRY CHECKED THE calendar. It was December 19. All of a sudden, the thought came into his head *Leda and I should get married on Christmas day! He* stood there transfixed. He tried to push the thought out of his head, but it kept coming back. That evening after work, he called Leda. She was staying at Suzie's for now. When they met for coffee later at the café, Harry gave her a big hug and kiss. He wasn't quite sure how to go about proposing marriage to Leda. He was fidgety and restless.

"What's going on, Harry? What's the matter?"

"Well, ah... ah..." Harry struggled to speak. "Ah... I wondered if you would marry me?" There, it was - out! He held her hand tightly and held her gaze. She first looked shocked but then a big smile spread over her whole face. "Oh Harry! I would love to marry you! I thought you'd never ask!" Harry gulped, "You did? You will? Really?" He jumped up and gave her a big hug and kiss. "Let's get out of here! We need to talk."

At Harry's apartment, they sat together on the couch in silence for a few minutes. Harry was almost overcome with happiness. All he could think of to say was, *"Thank you Lord! Thank you, Lord!"*

Leda sat quietly, as if she was struggling with something. At last, she said, "Harry, are you sure you want to marry me? I mean, you know what happened to me. I'm not a pure woman anymore. I might not be able to love you like you need." Tears flowed freely.

"Honey, do you think *I'm* pure?? I don' know why those bad things had to happen to you. I don't understand anythin'. I just know I want to marry you. We need to be together. God brought you back to me and I need to take care of you now. I had an idea the other day but was afraid to tell you. Ah... what do you think of getting married on Christmas day?"

Leda sat up and stared at him. "Christmas day? That's only five days away! Are you crazy?"

Harry shrugged and waited for her to grasp the idea. She sat for a long time, obviously battling with her thoughts. He walked into the kitchen and proceeded to make a cup of tea. Leda didn't follow him. When he handed her the mug, she held it tightly, like she needed the warmth to comfort her. Harry sat down and waited. He was having a hard time being patient, but he knew this was a monumental decision for both of them, not the least, for Leda.

"I don't know, Harry. I just don't know! I'm the practical one. I don't have a job; I don't have anything to offer you. I guess I can cook and clean, but that's not what you need. You need a wife to stand beside you and be your helper wherever God puts us. I need some help dealing with the trauma I've been through. I'm not sure I can handle something as huge as marriage right now. My emotions are so up and down. One minute I'm happy and the next doubt and fear push me into a big depression. I think we need to talk to Pastor Nick about this."

Harry thought for a long time. "Yeah, you're probably right. You've been through a lot. I'm tryin' to understand and tryin' to know how to help you." He hugged her close and began to pray, "Lord Jesus, you know about us. We know you love us, and we know you care about every part of our lives. Jesus, we want to do Your will and not ours".

They sat quietly, in each other's arms. Leda straightened up and faced Harry. She caressed his face and began to speak. "Harry, you know I love you. I know that Jesus rescued me from a terrible situation for a reason. Right now, I want to marry you with my whole heart, but I'm scared. Scared of the future, scared of how I'll cope with any stress that comes up. It's all well and fine to say I trust the Lord, but when it comes down to the real, everyday living and especially with a man, it scares me. It's nothing against you. It's just reality. Can you understand?"

Harry nodded but hung his head. Sadness overwhelmed him. *Lord, this isn't the way it was supposed to be. We had everythin' goin' for us. Why did this have to happen?*

"Okay, Leda. I'll try to understand, and I'll wait 'till you can get your thoughts sorted out. In the meantime, we still can celebrate Christmas! We still have each other, which didn't seem possible even a week ago. And we have Jesus! That's the most important part!"

Leda smiled through her tears. "Thank you, dear Harry! Thank you! Yes, Jesus is with us, and He will work everything out in His time."

Getting To Know
Ole Johnny

ON CHRISTMAS DAY, Harry and Leda were invited to share it with Ron and Betty and their family who were visiting. They had an extra special day, celebrating the birth of Jesus and most of all celebrating the safe return of Leda. After the big meal, Harry and Leda went for a walk. The air was crisp, cold, and bright with sunshine. They walked down the street where Ole Johnny lived. Harry suddenly thought that maybe Ole Johnny wasn't having a very nice Christmas alone. They knocked on the back door. "Merry Christmas, Johnny!"

Ole Johnny stood in the doorway, his disheveled clothes and hair indicated he had been sleeping. "Oh. Hi Harry. Wasn't expecting visitors. But do you and your lady want to come in?" He opened the door wider and motioned toward the kitchen.

Leda saw all the dirty dishes on the table and counter caked with dried up leftovers. Her first urge was to start cleaning up, but she knew that wasn't why they were in this house. The cleanup would wait.

"Johnny, this is my girlfriend, Leda. Remember I told you how she disappeared? Jesus brought her home to me in time for Christmas."

Ole Johnny extended his hand in greeting. "Pleased to meet you. I've heard about you from Harry. Please have a chair."

"I've heard about you too, from Harry! How you helped him out when he was having a hard time. God bless you!"

They sat for a couple of minutes, none of them knowing what to say next. Harry decided to ask Ole Johnny about how Christmas was years ago, when his wife was still with him. Ole Johnny seemed reluctant to talk about Matilda at first, but then he got going, telling them about a special Christmas time when they found out they were going to have a baby. They were so excited! Back then, Matilda went to church, and he went with her once in a while, maybe on Christmas or Easter. Matilda was so thankful to be pregnant, she was bouncing with joy. He had to admit he was thrilled too. Just thinking about being a dad was both scary and exciting. She had made a huge turkey dinner, and they even invited a cousin and his family from another town nearby. The little kids made the day complete. Then Ole Johnny's face went sad, and he stopped talking. Harry and Leda waited. "This part is hard, not sure I want to talk about it."

"Well, you don' have to if you don't want to."

Johnny heaved a big sigh and continued. "We had our baby in the summer. She was so beautiful! Dark brown hair and beautiful brown eyes. A perfect little girl. Matilda said she was an angel, a gift from God. We loved little Emily so much!" Tears ran freely. "When she was six years old, she was beginning to know her letters and numbers and getting all excited about going to school. Then she got sick." Another pause. "She got pneumonia and...and...she died!" Sobs wracked his whole body.

Leda got up and put her arm around his shoulder and Harry put a hand on his arm. They were all silent, lost for words. Harry felt he should pray. "Lord Jesus, you see the pain and sorrow that Ole Johnny has got in his heart. You know and understand much better than Leda and I could ever understand. Please bring peace and love to our friend here. He needs your special care."

"Thank you for sharing with us Johnny." Leda patted his shoulder. "It might have happened a long time ago, but the pain is still there, isn't it?" Ole Johnny nodded. "We'd like to be your friends, Johnny, maybe come by once a week and have a cup of coffee with you. What do you think of that?"

Johnny looked up at Leda with an expression of wonder. "You would do that for me? Why?"

'Well, it's like this," Harry chimed in, "We've felt the love of Jesus so strong these last months. We want to share that love with you 'cause we know Jesus loves you too. We've also learned about trustin' Jesus no matter what's happenin' around us. We've found peace where there wasn't a whole lot of reason to have peace, but Jesus has promised to never leave us, and he hasn't."

Leda grinned at Harry and nodded in agreement. "We need to get going, but it's been great to see you. We'll come next Thursday, okay? Merry Christmas!"

"Thank you. Thank you for stopping by. Yes, that would be fine. Merry Christmas to you too!"

Planning for the Future

IN MID-APRIL, HARRY and Leda found themselves involved in a couple of ministries through the church care group. They enjoyed reaching out to those who were hurting, lonely, or looking for answers to life's problems. Leda was able to get another job in a better paying restaurant and to settle in a new apartment. Harry, in the meantime worked at Percy's lumber yard, and became one of his best employees. Percy trusted him to deal with new customers and to complete the transactions. That freed Percy up to attend to ordering new products and supplies. Harry prayed every morning before work, that he could share the love of Jesus with whoever came into the store that day.

Harry and Leda talked more and more about marriage. Leda was going to counselling for the trauma she had experienced and recovery, though slow, was progressing..

"How about a summer wedding?" She asked one day, out of the blue.

Harry wasn't expecting the question and looked at her in amazement. "Really? Summer? Why not? Maybe June?" He couldn't wait to make more plans.

Leda laughed at his eagerness. "Yes, I've been thinking of June, too. Are we having a small wedding or a great big party?"

They were on their way to see Ole Johnny. They looked forward to their visits with him every week and were getting to know him better. He would even let Leda make the coffee and clean the kitchen. "Hi, Johnny! How are you today?" Harry yelled in the door.

"Come in. Come in! Welcome!"

When they were seated at the table, Johnny asked, "What's going on? You guys are looking pretty excited. Are you going to let me in on it?"

Leda giggled like a schoolgirl, "We just decided we're going to get married in June. What do you think of that?"

"It's about time! Thought you guys were never going to make up your minds. Congratulations!"

Harry noticed a mischievous grin on Leda's face and wondered what she was up to now.

"Johnny, I just had an idea - that is if Harry agrees." She gave a questioning look at Harry. He didn't know what she was talking about but indicated he agreed. "Johnny, would you walk me down the aisle? I don't have a dad or uncle around who would be able to do it. I'd love it if you would consider it." Johnny sat there; tears started running down his cheeks. Harry was overwhelmed. Who better to sit in for Leda's dad?

Johnny struggled for words. "Leda, you've become like a daughter to me over these months and you know how I miss my own girl. I'd be honoured to sit in for your Dad." He stood up and gave her a big hug.

"Thank you, Johnny, that means a lot to me too."

Harry went over to the counter and made some tea for them. At the table Harry suggested they read a verse from the Bible. It had become a regular routine for them to read and pray with Johnny and he didn't protest. In fact, he seemed to like it. "Johnny, today our verse is from Proverbs 18:22 'He who finds a wife, finds a good thing, and obtains favour from the Lord.' This verse proves to me that God is the one who designed marriage and He knows I sure need a wife! I've been roaming this ole world for a lotta years, lonely and lost. But since the Lord brought Leda into my life, I finally understand that a wife is a good thing. Guess you knew about that when you were married, right?"

Johnny nodded. "Yep, I sure miss my Matilda, she was a good woman. We had our spats, but that's life. We always made up and moved on. I got some advice for you two. Life will throw some curves at you in the form of arguments, fights, or just little disagreements. Don't let them sit there and grow, tend to them right away. That's how Matilda and I made it work. And remember, just because you've got 'religion' doesn't mean everything is going to be roses. There's always some thorns along with the roses."

Both Harry and Leda knew Johnny was right. They had seen enough of life by now to know that things didn't always go the way they thought they would.

Digging into the Past

WEDDING PLANS WERE in full swing by the end of May. Leda's girlfriends were as excited as she was and got together to make decorations and plans. The wedding was not going to be big, just a small ceremony that included close friends from the church. Leda would have her friend Suzie as her Maid of Honour and Harry would have Percy as his Best Man. Percy had become more than an employer. He had become a friend.

Pastor Nick encouraged them to take some pre-marital counselling as well. They both thought that was a good idea, considering their ages and past experiences. "Harry, have you forgiven yourself for the past? After you asked Jesus to forgive you, then you need to forgive yourself."

"Guess I never thought about that. I feel ashamed." He hung his head.

Leda reached out and held his hand. "Why don't you just talk to Jesus about it, Harry? He knows all about your past and he has been with you and loves you, no matter what happened."

On the way home, Harry felt the attack of Satan full force. It was like the whole sordid past was being replayed in his mind. The good times and all the bad times mixed in with remembering that he had left his daughter. He took his Bible and prayed urgently to the Lord for help. He turned to 2 Timothy 1:7 *'For God has not given us the spirit of fear; but of power, and love, and of a sound mind.'*

"Lord Jesus, I need you real bad. I don't know what to do about this new problem. Guess it's not really new, is it? It's been there in the back of my mind forever. You say in your Word that you give a sound mind I need a sound mind to think this through and to make the right choices." Harry sat in silence and waited. He felt peace because he had committed it to the Lord and was able to leave it there.

At the next pre-marital counselling session Leda spoke up. "You know Pastor, I feel like we both must move on - we have to. Dragging all the hurts up just opens old wounds that were healed over. Yes, we have the scars to prove there was lots of pain, but scars don't hurt, they're just reminders of how far Jesus has brought us. I, at least, want to go forward. To use the pain and lessons I learned to maybe help someone else. That's what I feel Jesus wants me to do."

Harry nodded, "Me too, I agree with Leda. We have to reach out to others, not just sit here and wallow in the past."

Pastor Nick sat for a long time. Harry and Leda waited. "Maybe you're right and I was wrong to try and dig into your past. I apologize. You have great potential to help many people and I need to help you do that. To look to the future. Again, I'm sorry."

"That's okay, pastor. I know you was only tryin' to help."

Time to Celebrate!

OVER THE WEEKS leading up to their Special Day, Harry had shared Jesus with Percy in many different ways. They had long conversations over coffee and Percy began to soften toward the things they read in the Bible. Two days before the wedding Harry came to work as usual, but something was different about Percy. He could see and feel it. Harry had been busy from the minute the doors opened, helping customers with their orders. Soon it was lunch time and they had time to sit down for a break.

Harry looked at Percy across the table, "Percy, what's up with you?"

"What do you mean? Nothing."

"Oh yes, there's something going on. You look different. Come on, tell me."

Percy munched on his sandwich and took a big gulp of coffee. "I've been thinking about all the stuff you've been telling about Jesus, I've been reading that magazine you gave me with the book of John in the back. It finally sank into this thick skull of mine. Last night I made the decision to repent and to give myself over to Jesus!" He broke into a huge grin.

Harry almost choked on his cookie in his haste to shout, "Praise God! Thank you, Jesus!" He gave Percy a hug that almost smothered him. They both wept on each other's shoulders. "Now you can really be my best man! Oh! God is so good! I'm so blessed!"

They had a hard time getting back to work after lunch. Both of them were smiling so much, customers felt the happiness in the place and seemed to catch it as well.

The evening of the rehearsal, the wedding party assembled at the church. They went through the whole ceremony, except the saying of the vows. Even Ole Johnny was there, so he'd know what to do. Betty and Ron looked after the details of getting the wedding dinner setup and the care group assisted.

The morning of June 5th dawned dull and rainy, but Harry was so excited he didn't even notice. At the church he looked for Leda, but remembered he wasn't supposed to see her until she walked down the aisle. Percy and Ole Johnny tried to keep Harry busy with small details, like, where was the ring? Harry pulled it out of an inside pocket and handed it to Percy. "Here, you better keep it, I might drop it or something. Is it time yet? What's taking so long?"

"Harry, settle down. It always takes a woman a long time to get ready. Better get used to it." Johnny chuckled.

Pastor Nick hurried into the room, "It's time! Let's go!" Johnny made a quick exit and went to the back of the church.

The others followed in single file into the sanctuary. Harry stood beside the pastor, and Percy to Harry's left. Harry kept looking for Leda, but all he could see was closed doors at the back of the room. Then a little girl and boy came in, walking hand in hand. Next Suzie came in wearing a pale blue dress and carrying a small bouquet of mixed flowers. Harry strained to see where Leda was. Then he saw her! She walked close to Ole Johnny, her face glowing. Her cream-coloured dress accented her light brown hair. She wore a small hat and carried a bouquet of three red roses.

Harry was convinced that he had never seen such a beautiful woman in his life. He was so overwhelmed that he could hardly keep his composure. When Johnny gave Leda's hand over to Harry's, an electric current surged through him. Leda looked up at him with a shy smile. They stood holding hands waiting for Pastor Nick to speak.

The Pastor focused on God's special love and how He had brought Harry and Leda through many hard times. He also told them he was convinced that God was going to lead them forward into an exciting future with Him.

Vows were said, rings exchanged, and the wedding party went to a side table to sign the register while Betty and Ron sang a duet. Then Harry and Leda were introduced to the congregation as "Mr. and Mrs. Bearpaw." Everyone cheered and clapped as they walked down the aisle.

Friends greeted them with hugs and good wishes in a receiving line. Afterwards, Rhonda was in charge of taking some formal photos of the bride and groom. The reception was catered by the church ladies and featured cold cuts, veggies and fruit trays with strawberry shortcake for dessert. It was a fun time of teasing, laughing, and speeches. Harry bashfully stood and thanked God first, for bringing Leda into his life. Then he thanked Pastor Nick and Rhonda and Betty and Ron, for all their love and support. Cutting of the wedding cake followed. Soon the party was over, and Harry and Leda went to change into something more comfortable before they left on a short honeymoon.

Harry could hardly believe he had Leda all to himself for a few days. Percy had kindly loaned them his truck and they had managed to save up enough money to go to a small motel located on a nearby lake. Harry's emotions were overwhelming him when he thought about how close he had come to losing this special woman. He thanked God over and over and vowed to treasure her for all his days. They had time to relax and enjoy their new relationship without the pressures of daily living while they talked about the future and prayed for clear direction.

A New Life, A New Routine

BACK AT HOME, the small group friends helped them move their combined households into a new apartment. Duplicate items were sent to a Thrift Store. Harry continued to work for Percy and Leda was able to get a different job working in an office instead of being on her feet all day. Her friendly, out-going personality was an asset as a front receptionist and endeared her to co-workers and clients alike.

Life settled into a routine of work, church, and learning to live together. They soon found out that what Ole Johnny had said about running into problems in marriage was proving to be true. Differences of how to do a certain task, or how each of them looked at a problem ended up in tense discussions at times.

Harry conceded, "Guess being older when a guy gets married makes for some extra challenges because I'm set in my ways. Sorry, honey, I've got a lot of rough edges that need to be smoothed down."

"Me too, but we are going to make this work, I don't want to ever live alone again!" Her face showed a determined resolve, and the glint in her blue eyes reminded Harry he too was done with wandering and living alone

The End
OR
is it the Beginning?

To order more copies of this book, find books by other Canadian authors, or make inquiries about publishing your own book, contact PageMaster at:

PageMaster Publication Services Inc.
11340-120 Street, Edmonton, AB T5G 0W5
books@pagemaster.ca
780-425-9303

catalogue and e-commerce store
www.PageMasterPublishing.ca/shop

About the Author

ISABEL DIDRIKSEN LIVES in central Alberta. She is a mother and grandmother. She worked as a Registered Nurse in Home Care until her retirement in 2001. She enjoys writing poetry and short stories. Hobbies include reading, listening to light classical and gospel music. Isabel has a special place in her heart for First Nations people.